The Dictionary of Missing Time

Susan Eileen

The Dictionary of Missing Time

The Light of Recovery Series

Halo
PUBLISHING
INTERNATIONAL

alo
PUBLISHING
INTERNATIONAL

Halo Publishing International
7550 WIH-10 #800, PMB 2069,
San Antonio, TX 78229

First Edition, January 2024
ISBN: 978-1-63765-514-6
Library of Congress Control Number: 2023918507

The information contained within this book is strictly for informational purposes. Unless otherwise indicated, all the names, characters, businesses, places, events and incidents in this book are either the product of the author's imagination or used in a fictitious manner. Any resemblance to actual persons, living or dead, or actual events is purely coincidental.

Halo Publishing International is a self-publishing company that publishes adult fiction and non-fiction, children's literature, self-help, spiritual, and faith-based books. We continually strive to help authors reach their publishing goals and provide many different services that help them do so. We do not publish books that are deemed to be politically, religiously, or socially disrespectful, or books that are sexually provocative, including erotica. Halo reserves the right to refuse publication of any manuscript if it is deemed not to be in line with our principles. Do you have a book idea you would like us to consider publishing? Please visit www.halopublishing.com for more information.

To My Mother,

Thank you for instilling in me a love of learning that has literally saved my life. In my darkest hours, I turned to reading and writing to escape poverty, abuse, and alcoholism. I researched my way out of my problems and was lucky that it worked. I couldn't have done that without the time and effort you put into my education. I remember how you sat down with a book, when time actually allowed, and ignored all of us. You were so happy after reading a good book that I needed to find out what was in those pages. And find out I did. I found the quirky, the eccentric, the plain, and the eerie. I found it all and then created my own.

My only wish is that you were here to see this moment. But that might be you—the cardinal that sits outside my window. Wherever you are, know that you had such a positive legacy that didn't fully reveal itself until years after your death, and I suspect your legacy is continuing to unfold through me, my brothers, and your grandchildren. It's such a testament to the quality of your character and spirit, which seemed to be overshadowed at times when people were distracted from seeing you as the role model you could be.

I am truly grateful that I had you for as long as I did.

Susan Eileen

Until the lion learns how to write, every story will glorify the hunter.
—African Proverb

Contents

A Reverse Kafka

Definition:
When someone gets their life together (for example, what happens after you get sober); the opposite of what is described in The Metamorphosis *by Frank Kafka.*

Exemplification of usage:
Rose is in recovery now, and during the last election was voted in as a city council member. She pulled a reverse Kafka!

In 1915, Frank Kafka wrote *The Metamorphosis*. In this novella, a travelling salesman named George wakes up to find that he has been turned into a cockroach. He's left to die in his room with only his sister, Grete, willing to bring him food. Once he's become a cockroach, he only likes his food rotten. Eventually, his family considers him a burden, and he allows himself to die of starvation—a slow suicide, if you will. Pretty grim, huh?

Alcohol provided the means for me to become a cockroach, but sobriety allowed me to perform a reverse Kafka on my life. One morning, I woke up realizing I would die alone in a room, like George. But life is like a remote; if you don't like it, get up and change the channel. So I did.

Once sober, I went from almost homeless to published author in two and a half years. But I digress. Let me take you on a long walk for a short drink of water…

When I tell people my favorite book is *The Professor and the Madman* and that it's the history of the *Oxford English Dictionary*, I have a pretty good idea of what people must be thinking. (I might add that it was the last book my mother ever gave me, so I'm sure there's some nostalgia there too.) Although it is about the creation of the *Oxford English Dictionary*, it also is about the Civil War and asylums for the criminally insane. As it turns out, one of the dictionary's biggest contributors was writing from an asylum. He contributed over 10,000 words!

James Murray was the editor of the Oxford English Dictionary, and he is considered its most prolific contributor. What Murray didn't realize was that Dr. Minor was contributing from an asylum for the criminally insane. Minor lived in America and joined the army right before Gettysburg. He became unhinged at the Battle of the Wilderness during the Civil War.

He was plagued with delusions of militant Irishmen coming to kill him after he was forced to brand a *D* (for "deserter") on an Irishman. One night after he returned to living in London, during one of these psychotic delusions, he killed an Irishman. This event led to a life inside an asylum, where he surely read the appeals for submissions to the *Oxford English Dictionary* and began his groundbreaking work.

The Professor and the Madman is an imaginative retelling of these two "inextricably and most curiously entwined" lives, framed by the story of how the Oxford English Dictionary came to be and the history of the making of the dictionary itself, which is more rambunctious than one would expect. Trust me, my life has been a series of rambunctious events and is now being told as a series of dictionary words.

Shakespeare didn't use a dictionary. The first English dictionaries appeared around the time of Shakespeare's death, and they listed only hard or choice words; the earliest were arranged not alphabetically, but by subject. The English language was spoken and written, but at the time of Shakespeare, it was not defined, not fixed. But as to exactly what it was, what its components were, who knew? It's ironic that the Oxford English Dictionary, now revered "as a last bastion of cultured Englishness, a final echo of value from the greatest of all modern empires," would demonstrate the degree to which English is not fixed, but endlessly changing. Today, it changes daily during this revolution of information.

Backing up a bit, in 2012, I noticed that words were creeping into my everyday language—*wardrobe malfunction, tot mom, humblebrag, Arab Spring, 99 percenters*. About a year later, during a trip to Cincinnati with my daughters, I—in a fit of almost rage—yelled at my youngest daughter to quit whisper bitching during our trip to the American Sign Museum. A hobby was born. I came across whisper bitching in *The Book Thief*. One of the characters had said something, and the description was that "it was a shout delivered as a whisper"—a fantastic description of whisper bitching if I've ever heard one. Whisper bitching became the first word in my online dictionary, metropolitanjargon.com.

I, like Dr. Minor, invent new words and have a dictionary of words for my life. At times rambunctious, other times funny, and sometimes hopeless and despondent, as life can be, this dictionary should be an insightful look at one woman's recovery journey. Reading and writing has allowed me to pull a reverse Kafka on my life, starting off as a cockroach and ending as a published author.

I'll let you be the judge of whether or not I belong in an institution for the criminally insane.

Pimp Spit Stories

Definition:
Stories that are over-the-top, possibly uncomfortable. and embarrassing. It's based on the Friends *episode in which Paul Rudd (Mike) takes Phoebe to meet his parents, and she tells a story about how she has hepatitis because a pimp spit in her mouth.*

Exemplification of usage:
I was on a date, and this guy was telling ridiculous stories about fighting—such as being outnumbered 6 to 1 and using a baseball bat in fights. And I was just, like, "Could we have fewer pimp spit stories, please?"

I sat there as the police counted the pills they found on me; they were trying to determine if I should be arrested for a felony or a misdemeanor. *If I get out of a felony, Lord, I promise I will quit drinking and drugging today, and I won't ever look back.* I don't know if they were playing a good-cop, bad-cop game, but I listened as they counted the pills I had stuffed in my pants and discussed for what crime I was going to be arrested.

I can't believe the turn my life has taken. Hell, I can't believe the turn this day has taken! All I wanted was a few anxiety pills so I could get some sleep, and now I'm possibly facing a felony! I already have an ankle bracelet on. I already have a swollen liver. Living paycheck to paycheck would be an upgrade at this point. Not only is my life not turning around in the wake of the divorce, but it is getting worse. Maybe being married to a cop had been keeping me in line on some level, and now that he was gone, I had become a total outlaw. If I didn't quit drinking and drugging, I was going to end up either dead or in jail, and quite possibly both.

There is a third option that I have been avoiding for years, and that is to get sober. I just might have to give sobriety a try. It couldn't possibly be worse than what I am going through now. But I'm so far gone, I don't even know where to get started!

***

The memory gets blurry after that, except that I was effectively scared straight. I haven't had a buzz since that day. I was on court-ordered sobriety at the time. There was an ankle bracelet on my leg that was continuously measuring my blood-alcohol content. What it didn't measure was if I had taken pills that day. Finding sobriety too difficult to maintain, I was abusing pills in the absence of alcohol.

The good news about sobriety is that you get to feel your feelings again. The bad news about sobriety is that you get to feel your feelings again. All the feelings that I had been avoiding for the past ten years were surfacing. I didn't know at the time that once the heavy, bad feelings passed, they would make way for true joy and contentment. I didn't know what I didn't know. As I sought to drown out and avoid the negative feelings in my life, I accidentally drowned out the good and happy feelings too.

You can't escape pain forever. Well, you can, but only from inside of a coffin. I had seen friends and family die from this disease. It's a horrible way to go. Seizures, skin that falls off the body as the liver fails. Yellow skin and perpetual nausea. Family and friends so disgusted with you that they avoid you altogether.

Getting sober was truly my only option. It was time to face the music. The fat lady was singing, and the lights were turned on. I was, like, the last person at the restaurant late at night—everyone whispering, "When will she go home? Doesn't she realize how rude she is? Doesn't she think about anybody but herself?" No, I wasn't thinking about anyone but myself. In fact, I was barely thinking about myself. I was only thinking about feeding the insatiable monster inside of me that wanted to run from the pain that I had been running from for years, and, ironically, all I was left with was more pain.

It was so overwhelming to think about a lifetime of sobriety; all I could do is take it one day at a time. I knew I wouldn't last in prison. I had never been in a fistfight in my life. My physical, mental, and financial health were nonexistent. My life was in complete shambles, and I was nothing more than a shell of a person. I didn't know how I was going to stay sober; I just knew that I was sick and tired of my own bullshit. I was on my own last nerve. I was tired of the lies, the drama, the chaos. I missed my sparkle days. I missed my children. I missed my promising future and genuine friendships. I was missing out on life. I was dying in plain view, and I was the last to know. Everyone but me could see I had a problem. There was no talking my way out of this arrest.

Even if I only get sober for a bit to placate everyone, I at least need to try it. I'm terrified of prison. I'm more terrified of prison than of sobriety—I've been scared straight. The fun times at parties and watering holes dried up long ago. I'm left with only the pain and the chaos I was desperately trying to avoid. Nothing to do now but go home, go to sleep, and start on sobriety tomorrow. Tomorrow is day one…the "one day, I will get sober" has now turned into "the pain of staying the same is greater than the pain of changing." I'm so tired of my own bullshit I can't stand it.

The police decided I was not in possession of enough pills to constitute a felony, so I earned a misdemeanor charge and was sent home.

I woke up in the morning, and the long day stretched out before me. I never realized how long a twenty-four-hour day was. The amount of time in a single day seemed unreasonable. I needed to assess what to do with my time. Well, first things first. My life was a wreck! I hadn't folded clothes in months, I was on the verge of financial collapse, and I was barely taking care of myself. I needed to treat myself as though I were barely older than a grade-school child—wake up, shower, brush my teeth, take walks in the neighborhood to burn time, and get out of my head.

Think, Sue, think! What did you do with your time before you were an addict? Well, you were married with children and had a job as a teacher, but that is all gone now. But what about hobbies? I used to scrapbook and read books by the dozen. I used to go to movies and check out new restaurants. I used to go on vacations. I used to do a lot of things. "I used to" is one of the saddest sentence starters in the English language. I used to have a career; I used to have a mom; I used to have a sense of pride. The only statement sadder than "I used to" is "almost." She *almost* beat the cancer. Our love *almost* weathered the storm. I *almost* got the job. My life had turned into a series of "used tos" and "almosts."

But I was turning all that around. I was taking as many suggestions as I could get. My oldest daughter introduced me to Pinterest. It was free fun for hours, envisioning how I was going to redecorate once I got my shit together. The recipes gave me the motivation to cook again.

My brother advised that the only way to get my finances in order was to assess where I was and start from there. How much debt did I have? What was the true picture of my income? What common budgeting mistakes was I making? The only way to create a budget was to track my money for a month or two in order to create a realistic budget for the future.

I picked up local maps to nearby parks. Again, I tried a twelve-step program with no success—my sponsor thought she could tell me to stop taking my mood stabilizers, and I knew full well that stopping those medications would leave me institutionalized.

The five-step program and sobriety coaching I found online was the final piece of my sobriety puzzle. I kept putting one foot in front of the other and hoping for the best. This was my only logical option. The other two options were prison or death.

Eventually, my hands stopped shaking. I began sleeping through the night. The world didn't seem oppressively overwhelming. The noises didn't seem too loud anymore; the sun didn't seem too bright. I had dulled my senses for so long that sobriety was overstimulating. Lying in my bed at night, I wound down with a good book.

As I peacefully drifted off to sleep with my book in hand, I could hear Frank stumbling around in the living room downstairs. He's never going to get sober. There's no way I'm going to stay sober with him around. I've got to rip the Band-Aid off on yet another relationship. Recovery is a selfish program, and the only way I'm making it out alive is to get rid of Frank. He's a level of dysfunction that has become intolerable. Instead of me helping him to improve his life, he will only drag me down to his level. When you dance with the devil, you don't change the devil; the devil changes you.

Breakups suck, but I truly have no other choice. I'm going to break up with Frank once and for all. The expiration date on our relationship has long passed. My friend Rose gave me a book, titled *Codependent No More*, with journaling activities. It gave me the hope of finding a healthy relationship one day, but this relationship is anything but healthy. In fact, this relationship is trying to kill my dreams from the inside out.

It's time to end this once and for all. But he's drunk now and won't think I'm serious. First thing in morning, though, it's time to kick this hobo out. Just because he doesn't hit me, doesn't mean it's not toxic. It's draining on every possible level, and not one of my needs is getting met. I'm just enabling him. It's not fair to him to him or me. Breaking up is hard to do, but when the bad times are far more frequent than the good times, there is no point in continuing this untenable situation. Despite how well I've learned to avoid conflict and ignore my own needs, I must do what needs to be done…first thing tomorrow.

Prosperity Preacher

Definition:
Those who preach in megachurches. Their motives range from highly suspect to downright unscrupulous.

Exemplification of usage:
Him: Can you believe that guy didn't open his church during that hurricane in Texas?

Me: What do you expect from a prosperity preacher?!

We arrived at my grandparents' house in the early morning hours. Suddenly and without warning, all five of us were living in one bedroom. It was culture shock without leaving the country. My mother had decided to leave my father; before dinner, we were living in Massachusetts. By dawn, we were outside of Cleveland, Ohio, in the upstairs of my grandparents' house. This was around the time Nixon was resigning from the Oval Office. Walter Cronkite was the most famous man on the news; the famine in Cambodia dominated the airwaves. The Vietnam War had recently ended, and the Kent State shooting had only happened days before.

Eventually, my mother was able to afford a saltbox house in the country. It was old and moldy, with plaster and lath walls. The ceiling leaked, and we had buckets catching water in our bedrooms. The wallpaper in the kitchen had tacky yellow, red, and orange flowers everywhere. As fast as money was coming in, it was going out. My mother was working as an educational aide at the local elementary school, but her drinking low-grade vodka quickly became a problem.

Saturday mornings were glorious as a child. We hunkered down as a family to watch Saturday-morning cartoons. The saltbox was growing more decrepit by the year. The living room, when the house was built, would have been known as a parlor; it was a long, rectangular room with a baby grand piano in the corner. Being the poorest relatives on both of sides of the family came with being gifted hand-me-downs from wealthier relatives. The piano was one of those gifts. Living in poverty but having a baby grand piano was the foundation for my personality that can be best described as a walking contradiction.

Stuffed into the erstwhile parlor was a brown, flowered, three-piece living room set, a large wooden console TV, and the piano, while a large turntable rested in the reading nook on the south side of the room. Growing up with three boys had me behaving like a tomboy, and Saturday mornings were no exception. The morning started off with all three of us huddled in front of the TV. My mother was strict about keeping us away from the TV during the week, on nice days, and for any other reason she could think of. According to her, TV started the decline of family values; when we were allowed to watch, we binged. Cartoons ran for three hours—duck season, rabbit season, duck season… That silly rabbit had us in knots for hours.

Mom was in the kitchen making us breakfast the way a short-order cook would. She cooked our eggs to order. My favorite was a scrambled-egg sandwich; being both the baby of the family and the only girl, I got my food first. The older you were, the longer you had to wait for food. I think she made single parenting significantly more difficult by over-catering to our needs at mealtime.

When the cartoons were done, Greg and I walked to the local corner store in hopes of getting a new comic book or Paint by Numbers. X-Men comics were my guilty pleasure, but I couldn't help thinking my body was subpar when compared to the glamorous mutants who graced the comic-book covers. Their bodies were curvy, and their hair flowed for miles. My body was as flat as the vinyl records in my living room, and my hair hung greasy and limp around my face. I couldn't wait to look as glamorous as Wonder Woman, or be as complicated and mysterious as Dark Phoenix. We fished the change out of the cushions in the living room and from under the seats in the car, and grabbed dropped change in the parking lot. Our search usually yielded enough money for a comic. We had to wait for payday for a Paint by Numbers or model car with which to spend the afternoon. When the money was more bountiful, I might even get a Hook a Rug.

After squandering our newfound change as quickly as we found it, we sauntered home to watch old movies until dinnertime. Black-and-white horror movies featuring gigantic eyeballs and radioactive spiders scared me from the living room. It was time to isolate and recharge with a good book. I would get lost in the pre-dinnertime book, oblivious to the fact that parts of the family were growing restless and sneaking vodka as the boredom of the weekend set in. The rest of Saturday was a gamble, depending on how much my mother exercised her elbow with the cheap gas-station vodka she picked up. By dinner on Saturday, I already had this ominous feeling that the weekend was coming to an end. Church was first thing in the morning, followed by an excruciatingly boring afternoon, and then back to school on Monday.

Catholic Church to me was like religious square dancing. In church, you repeat after the priest, one, two, kneel and pray, three, four, repent for your sins, five, six, shake your neighbor's hand, seven, eight... It was too formulaic for me to feel connected to a higher power in any way. It was sterile and unfriendly, rote and boring. The priest lacked charisma, and statues often seemed almost creepy. I was not a fan. But if I didn't go, I would rot in hell for all eternity. There were so many accidental ways to be eternally damned; I couldn't figure out how I was going to escape hell at all. French kisses, swearing, my divorced mother, and missing Mass were all sins that warranted eternal torture. There would be hell to pay Sunday afternoon if the receipt from God wasn't on display in the living room for all to see.

After Mass, the priest passed out pamphlets about upcoming church events—a receipt from God, if you will. I would grab the pamphlet and wave it around Sunday in front of my grandparents, when they happened to stop by, to be sure everyone knew I was heaven-bound. Can't start too early on a good reputation. The pamphlets were everywhere in hopes that my integrity would never be questioned. It was a superficial and transactional view of the afterlife, but that was all I was given to work with. If the road to hell is paved with good intentions, then surely the road to heaven is littered with receipts from God.

There was a sinking feeling that I was getting my spirituality all wrong. I was less than the sexy mutants, I was less than pie-baking churchgoers, and I was even the odd man out at home. This receipt from God couldn't have less meaning to me if it tried.

Sets the Table

Definition:
Actions that precede sex, that get you in the mood before having sex. Foreplay is the most important part of setting the table.

Exemplification of Usage:
Her: You seem so much happier these days! What's the secret?

Me: My boyfriend is great; he always sets the table with good conversations and candlelit dinners among other things...

In the fall of 1974, my family moved into a saltbox home in Northfield, Ohio. The house was old and decrepit, but it was far larger than the upstairs of my grandparents' home. Our blue Travelall was parked in the driveway. As we started to unpack, I spotted a girl across the field. I was so excited that there were kids to play with in my new neighborhood.

That family next door became my nearest and dearest friends. They were originally from West Virginia. The oldest boy was named after his estranged father. Next in line was Penny; she was three years older than I. Jessica, the girl I spotted across the field, was my age, and Sarah, the baby of the family, was in diapers.

Their white farmhouse was even more dilapidated than our home. It was rather large—three bedrooms, a formal dining room, kitchen, living room, and mudroom. The roof was in such poor condition that buckets were used to catch water, and the upstairs was unsafe to walk through. A ladder in the closet of the parents' room was the only way to get upstairs. The cellar was dark and damp, the remnants left by previous residents were abandoned down there.

The parents were rarely home; they loved to drink and gamble at the local watering holes. The father worked at LTV Steel, and the mother floated from job to job. By all accounts, they were more poverty-stricken than my own family. But I loved going over there for so many reasons. Avon catalogs could be found in every home in the seventies, and I loved the catalogs lying around. Their house was just livelier. Their mother scared me with her abrasiveness at times, but I always respected her. She had an "I take no shit" attitude long before it became popular.

At the edge of the driveway, the yard gave way to a steep precipice leading to the overgrown field. We played in that field between our houses all summer long. Sarah and

I made mud pies after a strong thunderstorm. We made plans to build an underground fort in that field. We played tag, chased butterflies, and got stung by bees in that field. It was our refuge.

During the summer, my mother would pitch a large, green, army-sized tent in our own backyard; we slept in it when the weather permitted. The tent was always pitched next to the tree of heaven that was in the flattest part of the yard. The yard belonging to my saltbox home was very spacious with many different types of trees. There was room to play baseball, have a swing set, a fire pit, and a garden, all in one yard.

When the weather was too foul to sleep outside, but not bad enough to force us into the basement, we slept on the porch. We were the feral cats of the neighborhood. No lessons in cooking or housekeeping, no help with homework, nor other such responsible endeavors. It was all fun, all the time, as childhood is meant to be. I adjusted to the extreme lack of supervision far too early in life—it was a recipe for disaster that would start brewing in my teenager years and pick up speed with time.

Whenever I needed to escape my house altogether, I went to Jessica's—my home away from home, not that her parents liked that arrangement. They were already struggling to feed themselves. Nevertheless, I hid out there to watch the TV shows I wasn't allowed to watch at home: *The Munsters*, *I Dream of Jeannie*, and *Gilligan's Island*. My parents only allowed me to watch PBS—too many commercials during these other shows. Commercials that would lead to requests for money, requests for trips to the store, requests for stuff. We didn't have money for stuff. Best to avoid the conversation altogether.

I had my first kiss in Jessica's house when I was in sixth grade. I knew this boy, Chris, had a crush on me, and I was terrified. I had no idea why a boy would want to kiss me, and I had no idea how to kiss. He kept asking to come see me. I decided to consult Peggy on how to kiss a boy. Peggy told me all about French kissing, which sounded way too complicated for a first kiss. Using your tongue, opening and closing your mouth, not being too aggressive, but being playful at the same time—how did other girls know how to do this?

I was getting more nervous by the minute. The song "Let's Get Physical" was the number one song on the radio, and I just wanted to stay twelve because I was afraid of boys. I didn't want to grow up, but time was marching on. More and more boys were becoming interested in me, and for the life of me, I couldn't understand why. Just last year, I was being bullied. Barely a summer later, boys want to kiss me? What was happening? I was too shy for my own good and extremely awkward. I was petite and about as demure as one could be. But when I looked in the mirror, I saw a gangly girl with a toothy grin, not the kind of lips boys wanted to kiss.

Chris, the boy who had a crush on me, was relentless in his pursuit of a first kiss that sixth-grade year. Chris was in grade school with me. He had almond-shaped eyes, feathered brown hair, and seemed to be as shy as I was. I knew next to nothing about this boy. Why would I want to kiss him? He was an enigma to me.

One day, after walking me home from school, he came to Peggy's house to watch TV with me. Peggy kept peeking through the doorway. After all the French-kissing instructions, I'm sure she wanted to see how it went!

Chris finally leaned in for my first kiss! I was nearly paralyzed with fear. Then it was over in a few seconds. I felt so relieved!

It must not have been that awful after all. Or was it? I never heard from Chris again. The walks home stopped. The chase stopped. I felt confused but relieved at the same time. I was left wondering what had I done wrong. Was I bad kisser? Did I have bad breath? I wasn't ready for boys, and never even considered if they were ready for me. I would need to muster up courage and self-confidence before my next kiss—maybe even more lessons from Penny.

I can barely breathe in the presence of boys, let alone kiss them, I decided. My nerves got the best of me. I wasn't willing to return a boy's advances…and didn't until high school, when I met my high school sweetheart. Before that, though, I kept filling my time with Barbies, Hook a Rugs and comic books. Boys were the last thing on my mind, even though I seemed to be in the forefront of theirs.

I had no idea my courage would later come in the most artificial of all forms, a liquid elixir I felt I needed to feel comfortable in my own skin, larger than life, and almost arrogant. The liquid elixir would be an overcorrection to my lack of self-confidence.

Four-Forty AC

Definition:
Four-forty AC is air-conditioning that comes from having four car windows down and driving at forty miles per hour.

Exemplification of usage:
Him: Bro, it's hot in here.

Me: Start rolling down the windows—I've got four-forty AC.

During my sixth-grade year, I took a road trip with my father. My father was a radio astronomer, a professor at UMass, and a part-time consultant at NASA. We went to California on business; it was the trip of a lifetime. We landed in Sacramento and travelled for three weeks on the road until we reached our destination. Airline travel was so very different then, but I learned a lot about his work in radio astronomy, and we stopped at out-of-the-way places that gave me a love for little and unique museums. At that time, my father was still living in Massachusetts, while the rest of us were in Ohio. We didn't get to see him much, but when he had to take a work trip, one of us would tag along. He was killing two birds with one stone.

First, let's talk about airline travel back in the 1980s. Believe it or not, it was a bigger dumpster fire than it is now. Nothing was on time ever. In fact, during our connecting stop at the St. Louis airport, I decided the airline that I was on, called TWA, stood for trouble, waiting, and aggravation. Who wants to be stuck in an airport for six, eight, eleven hours? Have you seen the prices? Could the chairs be any more uncomfortable? Can you be more bored and trapped? I also had to worry about bombs left by terrorists, hijackers, or just simply an engine failure that would prevent a safe landing. When they say that airline travel is safer than driving by car, remember that when a car crashes, you have a pretty reasonable expectation of surviving the crash. Not so much with an airline crash. Lockerbie flight 303 changed my mind forever on the safety of air travel, as did DC-10s and obviously 9/11. The DC-10 engine failures were a newsworthy story at that time.

It was the most time I ever spent with my father one-on-one. He had a PhD in radio astronomy. He was a pioneer in the field, actually. His obituary reads:

> *Professor (William) Dent was a key founder of the observational aspect of the astronomy program at UMass Amherst. As a graduate student at the*

University of Michigan, Bill had made the amazing discovery that the brightness of what were called quasi-stellar radio sources (quasars) varied with time. This required that the physical sizes of these objects be vastly smaller than had been postulated; many years later we have learned that quasars contain supermassive black holes, often with masses of billions of times the mass of our sun.

What were then called quasars, and are now called active galactic nuclei, were the focus of his work. He taught classes at UMass, did consultant work for NASA, and observed the universe from the telescopes at Kitt Peak National Observatory in Arizona. This particular trip involved contract work for NASA in California.

While on-site at NASA in California, I saw VTOLs—vertical takeoff and landing. Not quite a helicopter and not quite a plane, it was supposed to be the future of air travel. On this road trip, I also met a very influential man who worked at SETI, which stands for the Search for Extraterrestrial Intelligence. At SETI, astronomers look for radio signals that are coming from the universe, radio signals that might be coming from another world. We briefly stopped at Kitt Peak National Observatory in Arizona, where he did "observing runs" for three weeks every summer.

My dad was a very intelligent man. One thing I've come to learn over the years is that two signs of intelligence are wanting to be alone more than the average person and wanting to spend time with people more one-on-one. In fact, he was so intelligent that I feel as if he was too smart for his own good, often ruining his own happiness. He and my mother had four children, and I don't know what my dad thought fatherhood would be like, but being married with children did not suit him at all. It was far too noisy for him, if you want to boil it down to basics, and I don't think he was a one-woman kind of guy either. He preferred to spend time with us one-on-one; with sibling rivalry out of the way, he could enjoy our company. Only if everything was on his terms could he be happy, and often not even then.

We travelled from Cleveland to Sacramento by plane. There was a car, waiting there in Sacramento, that we then used to drive down the coast to Houston. We stopped at some of the most interesting and out-of-the-way places. One of them was the Winchester House of Mystery. I had seen it on the TV show *Ripley's Believe It or Not*; he must've made a mental note of my fascination and arranged for the trip. This attention to detail surprised me. He remembered how fascinated I was by this house on *Ripley's*, so he arranged for us to visit the home turned museum.

The Winchester House of Mystery is quite the architectural oddity. From the official website, here are the facts:

> *From 1886 to 1922, construction seemingly never ceased as the original eight-room farmhouse grew into the world's most unusual and sprawling*

mansion featuring: 24,000 square feet; 10,000 windows; 2,000 doors; 160 rooms; 52 skylights; 47 stairways and fireplaces; 17 chimneys; 13 bathrooms; 6 kitchens. Built at a price tag of $5 million dollars in 1923, or $71 million today.

It is believed that Sarah Winchester, part of the family that started the Winchester Rifle Company, was haunted by those who were killed by the Winchester rifles. The ghosts tormented her, she said. She was a beautiful socialite who withdrew from society and focused on her house of mystery. What prompted the constant construction? No one knows, but the construction continued until her dying day. There were stairs that led nowhere, and cabinets that were only inches deep. It's an expensive endeavor to build such unusable parts of a home.

This is where my fascination with unusual museums and unusual people began—with Sarah Winchester. Intuitively, I must've sensed that I had more in common with Sarah Winchester than anybody realized.

Although this trip was a special one, I found myself silencing myself repeatedly during the trip. I didn't want to make waves, didn't want to cause trouble. I was trying to be as agreeable as possible, at my own expense. If I didn't feel well, I suffered in silence, not wanting to put a damper on the trip. I did feel unwell often on that trip. I blamed it on jet lag and food I wasn't used to, but that wasn't an accurate diagnosis.

We drove from Sacramento to Houston over the course of that trip. The end of the trip came to a sudden halt, though. We travelled to Houston, Texas, specifically to catch the flight home. Little did we know that Houston had two airports, and we arrived at the wrong one. This is where the chronically late airline industry was actually a good thing. We had to drive across town to the OTHER Houston airport. Because nothing was ever on time, I didn't miss my flight home, even though we arrived at the correct airport two hours late. It was an experience to remember, and the euphoria coming to a sudden halt at the end of trip felt like whiplash, but we all have to go back to reality at some point.

At the airport gate, my mother was waiting for me with a winter coat in case I was cold when I landed. There is a big temperature difference between Houston and Cleveland. I was overly impressed with my dad for remembering that I was fascinated by the Winchester House of Mystery, and completely nonplussed that my mother thought ahead to bring me a coat for my basic needs. A pattern that I'm sure repeats itself in my life more than I realize. A zero-sum mentality about your divorced parents—you can only appreciate one parent at a time, as it has to come at the expense of the other.

Upon arrival at my saltbox home, my missed homework was waiting. It was lost on me that my father got to be the fun dad while my mother sat at home, doing laundry and arranging homework. Their responsibilities were off balance even in the divorce. The euphoria of that trip, however, wore off quickly, but its impact lasted a lifetime. Throughout the course of my life, I have valued travel over many other ways to spend my money; that was true long before I used travel to hide my biggest secret, which developed in adulthood.

Memory Burn

Definition:
A memory so unpleasant that you won't repeat the activity, and you prefer it be completely forgotten.

Exemplification of Usage:
Him: Let's do a shot of tequila.

Me: I can't—I got so sick off of tequila once that I will never drink tequila again.

Him: So it's a memory burn—I get it.

My first job was as a summertime custodial assistant at an elementary school in Northfield, Ohio. As work is a fact of life, I thought I would share some lessons about what I learned at my first job.

I grew up in almost abject poverty. Food was scarce, the electricity was always about to be shut off, and we received help from the government and church alike.

One program that the local government provided in the 1980s was a foot in the door into the world of work through a program called the Summer Youth Employment Program. It was designed to get kids living in poverty into a job that could alleviate the stress of living in poverty. It was 1984, and the minimum wage was $3.35 per hour. I was fourteen at the time and super excited that I could tell my friends I had a job! Remember, work was going to provide us with the American Dream, so I wanted to start early for maximum success!

Reagan was the president then, and many of the programs that were keeping us afloat were disappearing. As even many Democrats would concede, Jimmy Carter was an ineffective president; however, families that were living on the edge, like mine, suffered great losses during the transition from the Carter administration to Reagan's. Food stamps disappeared. Mental institutions were being emptied. The first mass shooting at a McDonald's occurred when a man announced to his wife that he was leaving to go "people hunting." The AIDS crisis was being ignored, and cocaine was flowing freely. Cable and music videos were new, and the decade was marked by a vapidness that can be seen in the music of the time. It was the most plastic decade I've ever lived through, and I came of age right in the middle of it.

As a job coach and career educator, I learned many lessons from that position; first and foremost was the importance of training new employees. People in leadership positions like to criticize just about everything from work ethic to performance, but what training do they provide? More importantly, are they modeling the behavior they expect out of their employees? If the expectation is to work smarter, not harder, do they model that, for instance?

I was assigned to wash the windows at the elementary school where I was working. Doesn't sound too bad. Or maybe, if you have struggled with streak-free windows your whole life, it does sound bad. This was the kind of experience that left me hating to wash windows for the rest of my life. Everybody has their quirks and idiosyncrasies, and this story sheds some light on why I hate washing windows to this day.

The school was a brick, sprawling, ranch-type building. From above, it looked like the letter E, and it could house many hundreds of students in a day. While it wasn't a behemoth of a school, it wasn't small either. If I had to guess, it was probably built during the economic expansion that occurred after World War II; buildings built at that time had flat roofs. Flat roofs proved to be a very bad idea, as the water just collects on top and seeps in eventually, costing more to maintain than any money saved at the outset.

My boss, Dale, was a typical Midwestern man in Ohio. He was overweight and didn't have much of a personality.

He was very quiet, which is why custodial work suited him. There isn't much to say when talking about the job of a custodian. You were given your assignment in the morning, and then left to do it for the rest of the day. This sounds great, but if you are trained well, it just provides a lot of time for mistakes before anyone catches on that you are doing the job below the standard that is expected.

Dale approached me one morning and told me that my new assignment was to wash windows. I had no idea, when he told me this, that I would be washing windows from the moment I clocked in, to the moment I left, for two full weeks! Two full weeks of spraying down the dust-covered windows, using a squeegee to remove the excess water, and finishing with a dust cloth to be sure there were no streaks. The adage "Cleanliness is next to godliness" left this country at least a generation and half ago; I wonder how many people reading this even routinely wash their windows! No judgment here if you don't; it's just a point to ponder!

So I was set loose on the windows of this elementary school, washing day in and day out for two weeks! I was as tenacious as any fourteen-year-old on their first job, and I was so proud when I finished. I went to inform Dale that I had completed my assignment! He probably was irritated on some level because now he had to figure out the next project to keep me out of his hair!

He went and looked at the windows. Not even pausing for effect, he told me that they looked dirty, and I had to start all over! They were streaked and not up to his standard. It came as a gut punch, as this meant I now had to do this job all over again. Two more weeks of washing windows from sunup until sundown for $3.35 an hour. This rote, silent repetition was not enjoyable. The lack of direction was irritating. Adding insult to injury, I had to share my paycheck with the family so we could eat. I had hoped to buy clothes from Kmart.

Several years later, however, as I was looking for my first full-time job after high school, I realized how beneficial this early start was. That custodial job led to fast-food positions in the area, and then I worked my way up to secretarial work before I was even out of high school. My first full-time job was a secretarial position at a private-detective agency, at the same time that Bruce Willis was playing a private dick on TV. This was the first real contribution to building a solid foundation for my life, and it was thanks to a government program.

By the age of nineteen, though, I realized that I didn't like desk work or custodial work. I didn't know what I wanted to do, but it wasn't either of those. Eliminating what you don't want is still part of the process, and my work career was just beginning, even if my work personality was still woefully underdeveloped.

Decade Barrier

Definition:
*When you are so broke that you can't afford
a car that was made in the same decade.*

Exemplification of usage:
*Me: I just bought a 2021 Chevy Cruze.
I haven't bought a car since 2006!*

*Them: That's great—you broke the decade
barrier!*

In the summer of my eighth-grade year, 1983, my father,
mother, brothers Bob and Greg, and I took a three-week
road trip to see the Grand Canyon. I recall the absolute
dread of going on that trip. I remember thinking how much
I would miss my best friends, Jessica and Sarah, who lived
next door. It was summer, after all. How could they take me
away from my best friends?

What eighth grader wants to hang out with their parents for three weeks, let alone drive across the country in a 1973 Chevy Nova? The car had no air-conditioning and was pea green. It was awful! Little did I know at the time how lucky I was to have my family, let alone the luxury of a three-week vacation. I got to see things on that road trip that most people only dream about, including hidden treasures that almost nobody knows about. My father was especially good at finding hidden treasures, and this trip was no exception.

On this particular vacation, we decided to camp at the Great Sand Dunes National Park in Colorado on our way to Arizona. This park seems to be a geological oddity. Nestled in the Rocky Mountains, there are thirty square miles of sand that reach a height of 750 feet. As a geology minor in college, I can only hypothesize how the sand dunes got there, but this is a camping story, not a geology lesson.

One aspect that I didn't anticipate, about exploring the West, was the scarcity of resources. It was 1983, after all, before the population explosion out West. Air-conditioning was not yet affordable enough for the mass exodus to the sunshine and heat of the Southwest. The availability of water and running toilets had been taken for granted by me until this trip. Unfortunately, outhouses in the raging sun do nothing for sanitation, and you're hard-pressed to find a place to shower unless you spring for a hotel room. However, as cities were hundreds of miles apart, the lack of competition drove up prices for everything, including hotel rooms. On a budget, we always camped instead of going to a hotel.

In preparation for this camping trip, I made a mixtape. At the time, people had cassette tapes for their listening pleasure, and many, young and old alike, played music on their radios and record players while transferring it onto a cassette. It was very tedious work that led to a lot of background noise on the tape. Slammed doors, screaming brothers, and radio personalities seeped into the recording. These mixtapes reflected your personality, though, although they did get old after a while. It was the 1980s, and hard rock was in full swing. To this day, I cannot listen to "Rainbow in the Dark" by Ronnie James Dio. I just heard it one too many times on that trip.

In late June, we piled into this green Chevy Nova, mixtapes in hand, for the longest road trip the Dent family would ever take. We drove from Ohio to Arizona, and back, in the span of three weeks. I remember the Grand Canyon; ghost towns turned tourist attractions, like Dodge City; and the Great Sand Dunes National Park. It's quite possible my love of rocks was cemented during this vacation.

At the Great Sand Dunes National Park, we pitched our old tent, also pea green, but family sized. This tent was a staple in the family for years. I don't remember much about the sand dunes, except that my twin brother and I decided to hike to the top of the them. We had no idea what we were in for.

Sand does not behave like a solid. This poses a unique situation when hiking to the top of a dune. Your feet are constantly shifting under you; you are constantly trying to find balance without falling over. It's quite exhausting for your body. Remember, some of these dunes are as high as 750 feet. As kids, we didn't realize that most people would not hike up 750 feet on a whim. As we had no fear of failure ingrained in us, we set out to climb to the top in the blazing Colorado sun.

Having a twin is a strange business. My twin brother and I have really nothing more in common than the fact that we were born on the same day, but people are so fascinated by twins! You would think he and I would've been on a constant play date, but as children we fought more than ever. However, on this trip we were forced into friendship.

That climb to the top was arduous, to say the least. The farther we climbed, the windier it got. The windier it got, the more sand pelted our skin, faces, and scalps. But we were proud of ourselves when we were done! We were kings of an actual hill, a sandy hill in the middle of Nowhere, Colorado. The windstorm at the top gained speed, so we were forced to return to our camp. Back at the bottom of the dune, we realized that we had layers of sand on our scalps, with no water to wash it off. We started regretting our decision, but how could we have known about the sandstorm?

Back at the campsite, deer were starting to find our food. Kids from our generation rarely knew what their parents were up to, and this trip was no exception. Oddly, I don't have any memories of my father at the campsite. I'm sure he was there, but those memories didn't make it into my mind. The trip to the top of the sand dunes is a memory that burns, though. I will have that memory forever!

I gained a love of road trips from these experiences. My tomboy nature and road trips made me very comfortable travelling alone as an adult woman, to a degree that I haven't really ever seen in anyone else. So much freedom, driving. You can anywhere, anytime—that is, if you are clearheaded enough to drive.

As my drinking escalated during adulthood, I drank at home almost exclusively. Too afraid to drive, my after-work cocktail turned into a type of prison sentence. While my childhood provided fun experiences, the nuts and bolts I needed for adulthood were as loose and shaky as the sand dunes beneath my feet; of course, I didn't know this at the time. I wouldn't figure that out until things went sideways one too many times.

Taste the Blackout

Definition:
When a drink is so good that you know you're going to drink until you black out.

Exemplification of Usage:
Him: How's your Long Island iced tea?

Me: I can taste the blackout!

The cellar in my childhood home was dark and damp, but for some reason, we were encouraged to hang out down there. While I was growing up, my mother routinely sent us into the cellar when tornado warnings came on the television. The cellar was the safest place to be during a tornado, she said. I think, most of the time, she just wanted a break from her children so that she could watch her soaps in peace.

In that cellar, there was a pool table my grandfather had brought to our house. He knew a bar going out of business;

next thing you know, it was in our basement. My first drink was down there, during a keg party when I was twelve. It was my brother's graduation party on a warm summer day at the end of June. The cellar stayed cool in the summertime—it was the perfect place to keep the keg. It was also perfect in that no one could see me sneaking sips before I was even a teenager. Immediately, I felt larger than life, no longer shy and awkward. The liquid courage made me feel good about myself in a way that nothing else did.

After that keg party, it didn't matter that I was underweight, living in poverty, and behind in hitting puberty. It didn't matter that every holiday I ever experienced was a clusterfuck of fighting chaos. It didn't matter that I never knew when my next meal was coming. It didn't matter that I was afraid of my own shadow. I didn't matter that all my clothes were out of style and didn't fit. It didn't matter that I was an outcast not just at school, but also at home. That drink made sure that nothing else mattered.

I was bullied at school for being too skinny, unkempt, and too well-read. By the age of twelve, I was escaping the only way I knew how. The quick hits of alcohol gave me relief before I even hit puberty. I couldn't make friends; I was painfully shy and truly embarrassed by my unfortunate circumstances. The alcohol made me forget all this and everything else that was weighing me down. That was the first of many unfortunate decisions.

In a truly misguided attempt to make friends, I stole makeup and took it to school to give it to other girls right as they were hitting puberty. This didn't last long, as I was arrested at the age of twelve for stealing clothes from the local Kmart. As I was escaping the Kmart, I was chased by undercover security and taken to the police station. I had to call my mother to pick me up. By middle school, the entire school knew I was behaving like a common criminal. Drinking, stealing... What's next?

My embarrassment over anything and everything led to that first drink in the basement. By high school, I was drinking Little Kings with a side of Percocet for breakfast. That first drink made me feel larger than life, pretty, and the opposite of a social outcast.

I began to self-isolate in every possible way to escape the chaos in my own life and in my own mind when I didn't have access to alcohol, which was often at first. After all, I'm nowhere close to the drinking age. When I hid in my room, I would complete Hook a Rugs and Paint by Numbers and write poetry. I was too smart for my own good, but not smart enough to not drink.

My first episode occurred in early sobriety, not surprisingly around the time of my first drink. I would conjure up ways to build robots, think about space exploration, and frequent the library to research these ideas. The fluctuations between insomnia and sleeping all day started almost immediately; my mental state was deteriorating. I had no idea what was happening, and neither did my mother. I was supposed to still be playing with dolls, but my life had been inadvertently hijacked by something I never saw coming.

This pattern would repeat on a loop for far too long. I didn't even have a car, a license, or a job. However, somehow, I thought drinking was a good idea. But it was just a means to an end. The answer to all my problems. It helped me sleep, it made me relax, it made it easier to speak, and it was helping me make friends, or so I thought. It was the magic elixir I didn't know I needed.

Budget Beater

Definition:
A car that you buy for an insanely low amount because the car has many problems, but it still runs for now. You put absolutely no money into the car and drive it until it dies—hopefully, no less than six months from the date of purchase.

Exemplification of usage:
Him: Dude, what's up with the car you bought? It's, like, three different colors.

Me: It's all I can afford. I can't afford a car payment, so I'll just drive this budget beater until it dies.

Somewhere in the middle of the Reagan administration, my mother started leaving the house. Where she was off to, I have no idea; I was just happy to have no adults at home so that I could have house parties. Just little parties with about fifty underage drinkers were what I had in mind. The drinking age was eighteen, so, to my mind, drinking at fifteen was only bending the rules a little bit. Considering some seniors in high school were legally allowed to head to the bar after school, it was no surprise that some of the younger girls dated seniors to have a few drinks on a night out. I found myself in that position sooner than I realized, and without even trying.

First things first, make sure Mom is gone for the night. She seemed fairly panophobic, but I suppose she did have a few friends. Next, copious amounts of alcohol, plus a cute outfit, are needed. Then, spread the word at school that I'm having a house party. Typically, fifty mean girls from school would be there, judging everything, and for some reason, I was trying to impress them. The house doesn't need to be terribly clean, just presentable.

Now, up to this point, I had lived in utter embarrassment about my living conditions. The house was built before World War I, so it could use some updating. The kitchen had bright-red, orange, and yellow shiny-vinyl wallpaper that hadn't been in style since the late sixties, but it was the eighties now. The ceiling leaked in parts of the house, and the sculptured carpeting in the living room was so old that it had lost its sculpture. In fact, it was best to leave your shoes on, even inside the house.

Because I was working on my high school popularity, however, I hoped that the drinking-with-no-consequences party would be enough to overlook both the shabby conditions of the house and my very angry twin brother. He had become quite religious, and I knew he wouldn't like this plan. All that "Honor your mother and your father" nonsense.

The saltbox home was on a large lot, one that was the bane of our existence on grass-cutting day, but a blessing on every other day. It had enough room to set up some tents, play a ball game, and have a bonfire. It had a wide variety of trees too—cigar trees, great climbing trees like maples, and a specialty tree that was referred to as the tree of heaven. No harm could befall the tree of heaven. The yard sloped down towards the backyard, leaving a swampy, low-lying area in back. When I was kindergartner, that's where the swing set was. Now that I was having keg parties, it's where the beater car got smashed before it was towed away. My friend Daniel's wreck of a car had been spray-painted with Sharpies the way a plaster cast is signed. I'm not sure how it got there, but once drunk, everyone beat the hell out of the car with a sledgehammer before it was towed off to the junkyard.

My twin was stewing about the shenanigans outside. He decided to set himself up by the kitchen door, monitoring all the traffic in and out of the house. People began arriving in droves—many more than I anticipated. The head count for a house party is always iffy. You just never know how many people will show up to bang a sledgehammer against a car on a warm fall night.

The alcohol, brought by the seniors, was flowing everywhere. I was too naïve to realize that they were just trying to loosen us underclassmen up for a night of fun, one they would deny the next day, disappearing altogether should complications arise. I'd been looking forward to the party all week; it was "bottoms up" in short order for me.

By that time, I had unofficially become a member of the stoners. I had dropped out of band. Even though I was still in honors classes, I was wearing the stoner uniform of skintight Jordache jeans and concert T-shirts. When we weren't at house parties, the mall, or the park, we were at a concert. The heavy-metal hair bands of the eighties put on a good salacious show.

The party was really ramping up, girls and guys were starting to pair up, and I think we all forgot to beat up the car, but my brother was on the warpath. He was trying to find our mother to tell on me, and for no apparent reason, he decided to charge my party guests to use the bathroom. As people left the house, they asked me why it cost a quarter to use the loo. This was beyond embarrassing. My brother was charging people for the toilet. Could our poverty and lack of couth be any more on display?

Someone must've refused to pay, because I heard a fight breaking out and Daniel say, "You don't need to be in Texas to have a chainsaw massacre." What was supposed to be a party good enough to get me in with the mean girls was now turning into a spectacle of public humiliation, and my twin was being compared to a murderer in a horror film. Once the fights started breaking out, everyone decided it was time to start taking off. Free beer and free love are great, but no one wants to get their clock cleaned for them.

At this point, my mother strolls in, all of us unaware of where she's been, and kicks the remaining people out. I yell and scream about my embarrassing brother, completely unaware that my party was an underage-drinking crime scene, but as a self-absorbed teen, I couldn't care less. I was trying to get through high school without being bullied every day. I was hoping to have some actual friends, but I was clearly going about it the wrong way. My mother was also shy and acutely aware of our poverty. She didn't like to mingle; she liked to read books, write poetry, garden, and such. I was asking the wrong person to show me how to socialize. She was afraid of her own shadow most days.

I was too young to realize that being raised by a single mother with four kids and a job, in a society that doesn't provide much support to boot, we were doomed to be, well, feral. It certainly had its disadvantages. As much as you may like the freedom of being feral, once you're in with a group of people who receive actual guidance from their parents, the differences in lifestyles really show. And that difference, with its baggage, picks up speed over time.

Square Dancing

Definition:
A code for married sex. Married sex is very mechanical and unoriginal—you do 1 and 2 to me, and I'll do 3 and 4 to you.

Exemplification of Usage:
I need to get some strange. I'm tired of square dancing.

I went to prom with my high school sweetheart, who later became my first husband. My high school senior prom was in May of 1988. One of my childhood best friends went as well with her boyfriend at the time. Prom was a much more low-budget production back in those days, while at the same time, the 1980s had a "too much is never enough" feel to it. The 1980s were very glam. The hair was big, permed, and hair-sprayed to death. Jeans couldn't be tight enough, and boobs couldn't be big enough. Cocaine hurricanes on the weekend were a real thing, and everyone wanted to be the wolf of Wall Street.

At that time, prom weekend in Northeast Ohio included amusement parks. We were lucky to have both Geauga Lake and Cedar Point within driving distance. We listened to music on the radio, and the local radio stations had contests for free admission to the amusement parks. They asked you to call in and vote for your own high school; the school that got the most votes received free admission to the park. My high school did win that year, and we received free admission to Geauga Lake Amusement Park for prom weekend. When they announced the news over the speaker system at school, we were all overjoyed; it was more about our school spirit, I think, than anything else.

Prom weekend was beginning to shape up. Prom on Friday night, Cedar Point on Saturday (another amusement park, but this was on the shores of Lake Erie), and Geauga Lake on Sunday. It was a curious time for drinking ages in the United States, as the drinking age had recently been raised, and there were different rules for everyone, it seemed. At the time of my prom, these rules were new: if memory serves me correctly, those twenty-one and over could drink liquor and beer, those nineteen and over could drink only beer, and for those eighteen and under, drinking was prohibited.

Of course, every girl wants to look her best on prom night. I was on a mission to find the perfect dress. The problem was, I didn't have much money. This was a simpler time, so we didn't do limos or nail appointments for prom. You found your dress, your hair was already curly from the perm, and you did your makeup yourself. We were not yet a service economy, so we did for ourselves instead of hiring others.

Of to the mall I went. It was Randall Mall, actually. At one point, I believe it was the largest mall in America. Two stories, a food court, little shops, some larger stores like JCPenney, and arcades. Where else would you want to be, other than the mall? You and your friends could window-shop, see a movie, and grab an Orange Julius. It was a great way to spend an afternoon.

So I went on a quest to find the perfect dress. Unfortunately, and this pattern would be repeated. In my quest for the perfect, inexpensive dress, I bought at least two inexpensive dresses. Did I save any money buying more than one? The dress I wore to prom was a white-lace, handkerchief-style dress. The bodice was snug and had off-the-shoulder teacup sleeves. I looked fantastic in the dress. I did splurge and have my hair professionally done that day.

Prom night was here. At the time of this writing, it was thirty-four years ago, so I don't remember much. We—Jessica; her date, Jose; my date, Mark; and I—gathered at my friend Jessica's house. We piled into my stick-shift Honda, and off we went to prom. It must not have been too exciting if I don't remember much! Formal dances for teenagers seem a bit illogical, but maybe that's just to me. We ended up at a motel In Twinsburg, Ohio, that night. For whatever reason, I remember that the room was thirteen dollars that night! Thirteen dollars! Curse you, Inflation!

Saturday morning, we geared up to go to Cedar Point on the shores of Lake Erie in Sandusky, Ohio. It was about a ninety-minute drive. I remember it seemed unseasonably cold that day, and a little too windy to be enjoyable. Such is Ohio weather. If you don't like it, wait fifteen minutes, and it will change. It was a very sunny day, and I had a bottle of Jack for us. Why we needed alcohol to have fun is another question altogether, but alcohol was already a steady backdrop in my life. We ventured out to Cedar Point, but our dates for the day had partied too much the night before. We didn't last long at Cedar Point, and we only rode a handful of rides. Before long, it was back home for the night to sleep. There was still Sunday Funday!

Sunday, we went to Geauga Lake Amusement Park in Aurora. Oh, the memories at Geauga Lake. This was the park that we got into for free because we had all called into a radio station because of our school spirit. So Sunday's admission was free, the hotel was thirteen dollars, and my prom was purchased on clearance. At some point, I knew how to cut costs! I need to remember those days!

I believe Mark and I were on our own on Sunday. We were well rested from the night before, and the day was perfectly beautiful. I could not have asked for better weather, and the fact that it happened on prom weekend was just pure luck. The roller coasters were fun, if outdated, and the water park was a blast. When we were done at the water park, but not ready to go home, that meant it was time for the beer garden.

Mark and I would have a shotgun wedding not long after prom night. We had a beautiful baby girl. This baby girl made me reevaluate my life and my priorities. I needed to get serious about a career. All I had was an entry-level desk job, and Mark worked in construction, which seemed very unreliable, but he was starting to have issues with his drinking. He missed a lot of work, always blaming it on the weather being bad or the car having a problem—there was always a reason he needed a day off. We had a baby; responsibilities were officially running the show, but we were basically kids trying to raise a kid. Not a very sound plan. I decided to enroll in college to get a "real job" after graduation. Way too many responsibilities, way too fast.

Witness Protection Program

Definition:
When entering a relationship, you blow off all your friends and family, possibly even your career goals, for the new and enchanting lover.

Exemplification of usage:
Her: I can't believe Monica has disappeared again! She met a new guy, and I haven't even heard from her in two months!

Him: It sounds like she's practically in a witness protection program!

Her: No thanks, to all that! I may miss a guy, but I'll miss me more!

My brother Tim attended the University of Massachusetts, starting in the late 1980s, where he met his future wife, Anne. Anne was from France and was attending as an exchange student. She went on to complete her doctoral thesis, but before that, they wed in July of 1991, and the Dent family went to France to attend the wedding. On the way to the other side of the pond, we stopped in England for a long weekend. It was the crown jewel of family vacations. My daughter and first husband didn't come with me, but I travelled with my father and my brother Bob, my mother and her boyfriend Martin.

I remember landing at Heathrow Airport in London as if it were yesterday. The culture shock was severe. I realized, by the end of the trip, that I could tell who was from England and who wasn't just from the shoes that a person was wearing. London was full of fashionistas who were ahead of the curve. I can say now that the shoes I saw Londoners wearing in 1991 would finally make it to the States some seven years later. The Midwest is typically behind in fashion, if it ever gets there at all.

The drivers in England drive on the other side of the road, aggressively, and during some of the worst fog I've seen. My mother's boyfriend at the time, Martin, also drove recklessly—he was the only one brave enough to drive in a foreign country, however, so I guess we shouldn't have complained as much as we did. The trip from the airport to the hotel was one of the scariest drives I've ever experienced. A white-knuckle ride, to say the least.

The food in London was downright terrible. I learned the hard way over the years that if you don't enjoy the food on a vacation, it will discolor the whole experience. Food is, after all, the most basic of needs. My brother Bob and I spent nearly the whole weekend in London trying to get a decent meal. We tried everything. We went to an Italian restaurant and ordered pizza—it was undercooked. We stopped at a street vendor for hot dogs—they were smelly and disgusting. We tried fish and chips—the fish still had bones in it. We eventually even tried fast-food franchises—the employees were washing the floors with bleach as we ate our burgers. The food was a total bust.

However, the sightseeing in London was incredible. The best of the trip was the Tower of London. It was once a royal castle and the site of a prison, complete with torture chamber. The medieval torture chamber was a sight to behold. We saw the rack—the device that would stretch a person and tear them limb from limb. This torture chamber was used as punishment for all crimes, both real and imagined, and even on kings' wives who were accused of infidelity. During that period of history, birth abnormalities were not understood. If there was a problem with the baby, surely the woman was guilty of cheating, and the baby's defect was a punishment from God.

Navigating throughout London was quite disorienting. It was my first time being in a country in which they drove on the other side of the road. It made even crossing the street difficult, as I was used to looking in the wrong direction for London traffic. Understanding the subway system, known as the tube, was even harder.

I recall sitting with an elderly gentleman in a local bar—he was from Ireland and more than slightly disgruntled with his life. We sat over a beer, discussing life in general and watching the movie *Body Heat* in a bar by the hotel.

At the end of the weekend in London, it was onward to France for Tim and Anne's wedding. I don't recall the name of the town, but it was in the rural mountains of France in an area known as Provence. The town was celebrating its 2,000-year anniversary that year. As you would expect with any town that is 2,000 years old, the streets were only wide enough for horses, and the buildings were antiquated. Anne's family home was there—we stayed there for the duration of our trip.

I'm not sure why, but, somehow, the culture of France was easier for me to adjust to than London. Maybe I had been shocked out of my American sensibilities in London and had had time to adjust to new surroundings, but France was much nicer for a holiday than London. It was sunnier, the food was better, and I was surrounded by family and familiar faces, after all.

The wedding was quite unusual, as compared to American wedding ceremonies, and I regrettably learned no French prior to the trip. I was barely keeping my head above water at the time, what with being in college, newly married to Mark, and Heather still a baby. The language barrier didn't turn out to be a problem at all, however, as the French learn English in school. I can remember a particularly good-looking cousin of Anne's joking that Americans were all fat from eating peanut butter.

At the wedding reception, the entrée was a pig's head full of other meats—what those meats were, I didn't want to find out, so I didn't partake of that dish. Dinner is served at around 10:00 p.m. in France, which at the time was considered very unhealthy. However, at the time of this writing, I've known many healthy people who eat dinner at this time, and certainly the French seem to be healthier than Americans. The dessert at the wedding reception appeared to be a bunch of pastries held together by some sort of sugary paste. Once again, I declined.

When I went to leave the reception at 11:00 p.m., I was told it would be rude to leave that early. I stayed and drank, kept pretty much to myself, and got lost in the mountains on the way home at around 2:00 a.m. I was a little more than tipsy, thousands of miles from home, and in the mountains of a country in which I couldn't speak the language. This smacks of a testament to my impulsivity—wandering in the mountains alone, drunk and unable to speak to locals if the need should arise.

After the wedding, it was time to return to a home containing all of the responsibilities that come with a life full of friends and family. Summer break was winding down, and it was time to get back to school. I was entering my sophomore year of college. Things weren't going well with Mark and me. We were just simply too young to be married. We had too much living left to do. Compounding that was his ever-increasing drinking problem, inability to find steady work, my indecision as to what I was even to major in, in college, and a daughter who was about to turn two. It was just too much without any sort of foundation on which to build our marriage and life together. Our foundation was partying until the wee hours of the morning. We were college age, after all. We were too young to be acting this old. As Tim was entering the witness protection program, I was deciding to leave it, but not for long enough, as it turns out.

Little Oppenheimer

Definition:
A narcissistic abuser who destroys every aspect of your life. Your finances are ruined, your mental health is destroyed, and even your friends avoid you because your romantic partner is that awful.

Exemplification of Usage:
David and I broke up a year ago over his narcissistic tendencies, and a year later, he's still harassing me. He's a little Oppenheimer.

In the spring of 1993, a close friend of mine and I were sitting in the cafeteria at the University of Akron. I was telling her how broke I was, that I needed money quickly, and I had no idea what to do. We came up with the idea that I should deliver pizza. I didn't know it yet, but this would alter the entire course of my life. The seemingly small decision to deliver pizza would land me in a relationship that almost left me dead.

I remember walking into Domino's as if it were yesterday. I've always been told that I look young for my age, and that day was no exception. When I applied, I was told I was too young to deliver pizza. I informed the manager that I was twenty-one, and he responded that I didn't even look sixteen. I went on to say that I was married, in college, and looking for a part-time job. I was hired on the spot.

Delivering pizza turned out to be a great job. This was during the Clinton administration—the economy was booming, gas prices were low, the nation was in a pretty good spot. That was nothing but good news for small business owners; my timing in working at Domino's was perfect. I was able to make my own hours, which allowed me to be around for my family when needed. The group of employees who were working there became like a family. We went to the bar together, had house parties, and went skiing. It was a blast. It was a motley crew of characters. There was Brian, the local Civil War reenactor and enthusiast; Sean, the player; Lisa, the young'un; David, the assistant manager; and Greg, whom we called Secret Agent because every question was met with a question.

This was before Google Maps; we needed actual paper maps to get around. No cell phones either—we still needed to use pay phones if there was a problem while we were on the road. It turned out to be good money, between the tips and the gas reimbursement. It was a way to keep my head above water financially; I made very good friends, and even met some future lovers.

I was still married to my high school sweetheart after what turned into a shotgun wedding. Those relationships usually implode almost immediately, and mine was no exception. As we were broke, the divorce was simple; we had nothing to divide. We were living with my mother in the upstairs of that saltbox house. It was clear my first husband was going nowhere fast, and what seemed like a small drinking problem quickly took over his life. I was not about to stay married to an unfaithful, broke alcoholic. I was in college and about to start a career in education. The pizza-place job was just paying the bills until I graduated.

David, the assistant manager, and I were scheduled together often; quickly, close-quarters syndrome was happening between us. Actually, it was Stockholm syndrome, but I didn't know it yet. He was married as well, but to say his marriage was rocky was an understatement. His wife was an alcoholic also. We both had one child. Romantic feelings quickly developed, although neither of us felt comfortable saying anything as were both married; an affair of the heart quickly developed nonetheless.

There were already so many problems in my marriage that I asked my husband to move out on a Monday during that spring. The next Friday, my husband already had his first date; evidently his foot had been already out the door before he actually left. David was also starting the process of his divorce. We started dating a short time later. Clearly, people thought we were getting divorced to be together, but our first marriages would've ended even if David and

I had never met. My first husband constantly accused me of seeing David while we were married, which was not true, but I was always confused as to why he even cared, considering he had been unfaithful during the marriage and was dating five days into the separation. It was just a pattern of mind games that would show up in my life more consistently than even my partners did.

David and I began seeing each other, and, right off the bat, I didn't like how fast David wanted to move the relationship along. Neither of us was technically divorced. I hadn't graduated yet. We both had issues to clear up before getting serious, but he disrespected every boundary, not that we knew what boundaries were at the time. I told him that talking about moving in together was too much, too soon. I didn't know, until after David and I were later married, that he took the "too much, too soon" argument to mean he should resume sleeping with his ex.

David was a secret asshole. He said and did all the right things to your face, but lied and was deceitful behind your back. More mind games. Someone who is an asshole all the time, well, at least is consistent. As is someone who is charming and pleasant to be around all the time. But being an asshole in private, but charming in public, causes your brain to be confused about which one is the real person.

That was the beginning of the narcissistic abuse, something that didn't even have a name at the time. It's similar to what happens when you put a frog in lukewarm water.

At first, the frog thinks this is nice; then the heat gets turned up until the frog is dead. It's falling in love with a silent enemy. A barking dog lets you know to stay away, but be wary of the silent tiger in the room. There's a perpetual sense of unease, but you're not even sure why. My intuition was telling me that the tiger would pounce one day, even though I had no evidence to prove it.

Before getting married, we continued to date without my knowing that we weren't exclusive, and I proceeded to let him walk all over me ninety percent of the time; it was a dream come true for him. We made plans to take a ski trip to Colorado for Christmas. On that trip, we discussed living together, but I told him that moving in together was too much, too soon. He responded with a marriage proposal. *This is level jumping*, I remember thinking, but it was more—it was coercion. Regardless, against my better judgment, I agreed to get married.

The fighting literally started on our wedding night. I put on a negligee, and he proceeded to tell me that I didn't look good in it—on our wedding night, he's insulting the way I look. He was asking for a divorce by day four. DAY FOUR!! This is a telltale sign of narcissism. They get you right where they want you, and then the devaluing begins. It leaves you wondering why they chased you if they're also trying to get rid of you. It's the beginning of your brain, your entire life, getting turned into scrambled eggs. The flame was just getting turned up under the pot of water I was in. I was mortified that he wanted a divorce, on day four, over a fight about passing the butter…and too humiliated to take him up on what would've been a good idea. If problems were showing up that quickly, it really had to be all downhill from there.

I graduated from college, but he still had no real career. He was still a manager at Domino's. He wanted to be a police officer, so he signed up for the academy. I, being both a good wife and complete idiot, paid all his bills while he was in the academy. He graduated and started a career in law enforcement. Now that we both had good jobs, we bought my grandfather's home; he was selling a Cape Cod not far away from the saltbox house. I was a teacher, my husband was a police officer, and we were living in a Cape Cod with our two kids from our first marriages. It seemed as if we were living in a Norman Rockwell painting. The American Dream was coming true.

But the explosive fights, the guns-and-roses nature of our relationship was escalating. There was no middle ground. Either we were getting along well enough that we were planning extravagant vacations, or we were discussing divorce. The divorce discussions were always on holidays or paydays—days that were supposed to be happy. I didn't realize narcissists love to ruin nice things, and Christmas, my birthday, or the receipt of unexpected bonus checks were no exception. For some reason, happy occasions brought out the worst in him. One year, he even cancelled Christmas, throwing the tree in the garbage, telling the kids that there would be no presents because he was moving to Canada. That was the worst—he was even abusing the kids. That fight started because he didn't like the tone of voice in a voicemail I left. It wasn't chipper enough. But if you ask him, he is the least abusive guy he knows.

By then, the abuse was taking a toll on every aspect of my life, and I started drinking to cope. I wonder how many women in psych wards or rehabs are the victims of abuse; it's a silent killer, I believe. There is such shame and stigma around it. I already didn't have a good track record with drinking, either personally or in my family; this abuse was the final nail in the coffin. The entire decade of my thirties was a series of stress-building events. My mother was getting older, my job in public education was getting beyond stressful, the kids were growing and had bigger problems, and my marriage was a war zone. By the end of my thirties, my mother was deceased, my job was gone, and David, now that I had no more money to give him, left me for being broke and having a drinking problem, all things he was instrumental in creating.

Even though he left me, he didn't leave me completely. He stuck around enough to scare other guys off, stuck around enough to abuse from a distance, stuck around enough to keep the destruction going—"I don't want you, but I don't other people to have you" mind games. I didn't realize it at the time, but living in this abuse was causing me to pick up abusive tendencies. I was getting infected with narcissistic fleas. I was turning into an abusive drunk.

I didn't even know who I was anymore, but I didn't like what I was seeing. My parents were pacifists. I had never been in a fistfight in my life, and name-calling was strictly prohibited as I was growing up. The volatile fights made me feel ill. I was becoming a monster. I was in love with a man who was incapable of committing to one woman; he would rather have three threes, than a good woman.

Getting into a psychologically abusive relationship is similar to moving into a centuries-old home that is haunted. At first, you think it's nice, it's affordable, and it's in the neighborhood you like. In your excitement, you move in. Within weeks, you know something is wrong, but you just can't put a finger on it. There are long-term invisible problems, such as termites eating the walls or lead in the pipes. The basement walls have cracks. If you try pointing any of these things out, you're told you're being nitpicky; they are small problems. Yeah, small problems that will escalate; you just don't know how or when. If you try talking to your friends about it, they say, "How do you know there is lead in the pipes? Did you see it? What makes you the expert on this anyway." You point out that you think there are more termites than you originally thought, and they say, "Why are you focusing on something you can't even really see. Are you sure the termites are there, or are you imagining things again?"

When you say, "I don't know. I can't put my finger on it; I just have a bad feeling about. There's something going on in that house; I just haven't figured it out," your friends say you're creating problems out of thin air. In your exhaustion, you decide to switch the subject entirely, but your women's intuition is telling you that things are not going to end well.

This type of psychological abuse is hard to explain, and it's even harder to define why it hurts so much. Like a white-collar crime, it's hard to prove, and even harder to punish. Even when punishment is delivered, it doesn't seem to be severe enough to fit the crime. I had difficulty convincing even myself that a crime was being committed. The fact that I had somehow turned into the very worst version of myself was actually all the proof anybody needed.

Drunk Envy

Definition:
When you see people drinking, probably not even drunk, but at the perfect point of tipsy, where everything is a little bit funnier, everybody is a little bit prettier, and the conversation seems to be wittier. However, you are in recovery, so you know that if you have one beer, it'll be sixteen more, you'll take a trip to the hood for some oxy, and wake up in a trap house, with some sketchy-ass chick. So you can't have even one beer under any circumstances.

Exemplification of Usage:
Him: Hey, what's wrong? It's a beautiful day for camping! Why so distracted?

Me: Ugh! These twentysomethings 'round here and their white claws! I'm feeling some drunk envy.

My career was progressing quite well at the middle school. Hired in at part-time, I was now not only full-time, but the department head as well. David's position as a police officer was secure, but he didn't enjoy his job nearly to the degree that I enjoyed mine. Although we were only in our thirties, he seemed to be counting down the days to his retirement. Both of our positions earned union pay; we were well-established middle class, if not approaching the upper limits of that. He still wasn't happy, of course.

To improve his mood and our relationship, we started taking scuba-diving classes together. Becoming scuba-diving certified changed the way we vacationed. In less than a full season, we were well-equipped to swim one hundred feet below the surface of the water. With our upwardly advancing pay, my summers off from teaching provided ample vacation time, and our kids were at a great age. So we decided to travel to Jamaica and try our first all-inclusive resort.

Jamaica was one of the most extravagant and enjoyable vacations I've ever been on in my life. It was my family's first resort vacation, and it was spectacular. It was an all-inclusive resort, with never-ending drinks and unlimited food. It was on the beach, but there was also a pool with a swim-up bar. Jamaica is a series of islands created by dormant volcanoes; the resort clung to the side of one the steep volcanic mountains. Our room overlooked the ocean, and there didn't seem to be a cloud in the sky the entire vacation. The locals crowded around the resort, hoping to sell you something the minute you stepped off the resort.

The culture shock in Jamaica was intense. Jamaicans drive on the opposite side of the road from what we do, they will jump into the ocean and catch a lobster to sell on the side of the road, and they live at a horrifying level of poverty. They leave their houses in a permanent state of construction, as property-tax laws state that you only pay taxes once the home is finished being built. I don't remember much about their monetary system, but I do know that the hyper-inflation led to stores called the "Couple Hundred Dollar Store." The drivers honk at people just to say hi and are beyond reckless. They speak what they call English, but it is a slang variation that was difficult to understand. It took a couple of days to adjust to the culture there.

Jamaica is a marijuana-friendly country. It is the home of Bob Marley and Rastafarians, so what else would you expect? The large mansions of drug smugglers were high atop the volcanic mountains overlooking the towns they were corrupting down below. I was there in 2005, and at that time, the United States was not very marijuana friendly. David was not a friendly person at all, let alone marijuana friendly.

The beauty of a resort vacation is that there is staff ready to coordinate activities inside the resort and outings on the rest of the island. We climbed a waterfall, went tubing through the rainforest, and explored the ocean while scuba diving. The scuba diving was disappointing, as the reefs were badly damaged due to climate change and pesticides. The tubing took us on a river through the rainforest. Red Stripe was the most popular beer on the island. The police officers are also called Red Stripes, due to the red stripes down their pants.

The island was full of people from around the world, and there was a "bar" for teenagers and a nightclub for adults. There were contests by the pool, karaoke, and a full-size chess game. The club activities for teenagers kept Heather busy, and Savannah was with a childcare service from time to time. The family activities were beyond comparison to other vacations I've taken.

Jamaica is a developing country. They speak English and drive on the opposite side of the road, but it is not unusual to see a person sleeping under a sheet tied between two trees in the forest. Possibly due to the lack of money for a social life, they do tend to sit around telling stories, not that there's anything wrong with that. With all-inclusive resorts, you never have to bring out your wallet. All drinks, food, and tips are included. Not having to bring out your wallet when you order drinks can lead to problems.

Back home, as I noticed my drinking escalating, I let my wallet let me know when to stop. But at the resort, since I didn't need to pay, I lost count quickly. I didn't want to concern myself with keeping track of drinks; I wanted to enjoy myself. The addiction math problem was starting to show up. How many drinks can I have before the night goes sideways? How many drinks can I have without ruining my budget? How many drinks can I have and not have to worry about a hangover? But with the wallet safely stowed away in the room, my addiction math calculator was not operational.

I was losing my Off switch—the Off switch that says, "You've had enough; anymore and you'll be unsafe to drive." The Off switch that says, "You've had enough; you have responsibilities at home." The Off switch that says, "You're going to have a 'shame-over' in the morning."

The line between having fun and feeling pretty was getting blurred. I woke up each morning and thought, *No, I didn't do anything stupid, I'm sure I'm just overreacting.* Within an hour after waking up, fuzzy memories started creeping in, letting me know that I might have some apologies to make. Some jokes may have been too crude. I may have been a little obnoxious. I was just hoping and praying that nobody was noticing that my Off switch was disappearing. *When I have free time, I'll figure out how to throttle it back. I was a social drinker for years. How hard can it be to get back to that good place where I don't have to worry about ruining the night?*

I swore I would never develop a problem with drinking as some of the other people in my family had. I was so much better than they were, anyway. I was smarter; I went to college, after all. I couldn't be similar to the family members who called from jail the morning after a night out. I couldn't be one of the family members who lost their dreams. I couldn't be a family member who never had a successful relationship with anyone. I don't know why I thought I couldn't be like them, but there it was—denying that I was like those people. Those were people I promised myself I'd never be. I was supposed to be enjoying my vacation, not ruminating on addiction math. The amount of head space this problem was using was pointless and got nowhere. It was a circular argument and, when looked at closely from any direction, always gave the same answer—the family problem has found you; you've crossed that invisible line into addiction. Only to argue with myself five minutes later that I was being dramatic again. *This is just a rough patch. Things will return to normal and settle down soon.*

The kids were enjoying themselves in this tropical locale. The pool was immense; the music made everything a little livelier. The swim-up bar had virgin drinks for kids. They felt so fancy drinking their drinks with little umbrellas garnishing the glasses. The American Dream was now a reality for David and me. Everything was coming together—the house in the suburbs, the union jobs, the three kids, and now fancy vacations with scuba diving and umbrella drinks. I couldn't believe how lucky I was. Going from a home with a leaky roof, and never knowing when I would eat next, to sunning myself in the tropics with unlimited food I didn't have to cook or clean up after.

David, however, had nothing but complaints—"The wild animals should be kept from hanging around the resort. Why do the locals expect tips? How expensive is this trip? What do you mean we're all sharing the same room? Ugh. Susan, I think you're turning into a drunk." The American Dream was here all right, but at the expense of everything I was trying to avoid from my childhood— drinking, chaos, and drama.

The trip even ended on a sour note, as David was guilt-tripping me into scuba diving one last time. I said my sinuses were bothering me, and it wouldn't be safe to dive, plus our youngest didn't really like the childcare. We hadn't travelled all that way to drop the kids off with strangers; we had come for quality memories that would carry us through times when we were nothing more than ships passing in the night.

That's when the fight erupted. Where were my priorities? Whom did I love more—the kids or him? If I didn't go scuba diving, that was it—we were divorcing when we returned home. His policy of instant escalation and the total disregard for my health were getting old. What did I see in this guy, anyway? No way we're going to make it to old age. The guilt trip over something as simple as having sinus problems seemed irrational and childish, and I was just starting to realize how impossible he was to get along with. This was supposed to be the trip of a lifetime, and now guilt trips, hate stares, threats of divorce over sinus problems?

Countless times, I tried explaining that this was unhealthy, only to be met with the argument that our circumstances were so much better than those we grew up in. Fancy vacations, union jobs, scuba diving—all seem pretty pointless when the lack of trust, loyalty, and respect were driving you straight into an addiction problem. Abuse is still abuse, even if it's wearing a bow tie, just as a white-collar criminal is still a criminal.

This is getting ridiculous. Why am I putting up this bullshit again? Ugh—I'll have a mimosa with breakfast. That'll turn the day around.

Second Shift

Definition:
The tedious parts of human existence that you must complete after you have already worked a full day. This includes food shopping, paying bills, laundry, cleaning, etc.

Exemplification of Usage:
Them: Hey, let's go hit the pub after work today.

Me: I really can't—second shift hits after work today.

Them: Second shift?

Me: All the crap you have to do at home after work; second shift is exhausting.

In 2005, my continual fifteen-hour days drove me to drink. I was married to a man who would never be happy. I swear, he could win the lottery and still be unhappy that he had to pay taxes on it. We all know people like this. Maybe you *are* such a person.

I worked as a public-school teacher outside of Cleveland, Ohio. It was an affluent district in *Suburgatory*. The kids were beyond entitled, and I was losing job satisfaction fast. I had three kids—two daughters and a stepson—and a husband. My life was jam-packed, but not fulfilling in the least. In fact, it was sucking the life right out of me to be around people who were treating me like garbage and wanting me to thank them for the opportunity to do so.

This was already my second marriage. What if I divorced David? Would I actually get married a third time? First, I married my high school sweetheart, but only because it was a shotgun wedding. We had a daughter. My second husband and I also had a daughter, and my second husband came with a son. Our family was right out of *Yours, Mine, and Ours*.

Blended families are rough. The first words my oldest daughter ever said to my second husband were, "My dad is bigger than you!" They were the exact same height, but she wanted to let him know where he stood. Maybe she sensed his ill intent.

My stepson isn't wild about me either, but there is nothing I can do about that. If I've learned anything over the years, it's not to force any relationship. If it works, it works. If it doesn't, it doesn't.

My youngest daughter was the happiest baby of the three. All three of my kids were my pride and joy—so much so that empty nesting a decade left an unbearable pain that took years to recover from. I tried to drink that pain away later in life. Drinking away pain doesn't work. You must feel the pain at some point, must go through the five stages of grief. If you avoid the five stages of grief, you will never get to acceptance, which is where you find peace.

But I digress.

My fifteen-hour days left me no time for self-care or unwinding at the end of the day. On top of that, the man to whom I was married kept telling me he was sick of hearing me complain about fifteen-hour days. This complete lack of empathy should have been a major sign to cut and run for the hills, but I didn't. His entire contribution was to just listen, and he couldn't even do that. His weaponized incompetence was something I had never experienced. I was convinced he intentionally messed up things I asked him to do because I wouldn't ask him to do it again if he was a total fuckup at it. He couldn't do household tasks on days that he worked, well, because he was working. He also couldn't do household tasks on the days he was off, well, because he was off and needed to recharge.

There was zero understanding that I needed recharge time too. There was zero understanding that I was a human being with needs. I was treated as if I were nothing more than an indentured servant. "Please don't whine about this, Susan. You should be happy I've given you this opportunity to know me and bask in my intelligence."

Second shift, and the lack of help with second shift, was killing my soul. I had to clean, cook dinner, do homework, take the kids to their activities, all by myself. I was helping to take care of my mother; I had papers to grade. There was no time for me. No time to read, no time for friends, just no time. I learned the hard way that you can't pour from an empty cup. If you don't take care of yourself first, everything you touch will fall apart.

I put off doctor visits. I wish that were the worst of it. I knew I was bipolar, but there was little understanding of mental health issues at the time. David told me it was all in my head—well, it sure as hell wasn't in my elbow!! Mental health problems are in your head! Along with childhood trauma and some bad genes lurking in my DNA. He was only focused on how early he could retire. Money was his God! If you meet a man like this—RUN! If you are a person like this—change!

I was trying to provide my children with a childhood better than the one I had experienced, and I was failing miserably. I was trying to be sure to spend quality time with them. One of the best experiences we shared was at the YMCA. For about fifteen years, I volunteered for various positions within the mother-daughter group known at the time as Indian Maidens. For obvious reasons, this has now been renamed the Adventure Maidens, but the experiences I had with the Indian Maidens provided my daughters and me with memories that will last a lifetime.

The Adventure Maidens had three basic activities–tribe events held at your home, nation events around town, and camping. We were in three tribes over the years and had great fun over the span of our fifteen years. We met monthly at each other's homes to do a craft activity. This is when my arts-and-crafts skills were on full display. One time, we made worry dolls out of yard and clothespins. Worry dolls are, I believe, a South American custom, native to Argentina. You tell your worry doll all your worries before bed and place it under your pillow. Once under your pillow, the worry doll takes over and handles your worries while you sleep. We did many crafts, colored eggs, and even had scavenger hunts, but for some reason, the worry dolls stick out among all the memories. Our mother-daughter events also involved cabin camping.

The camping trip that sticks out among all is our spring trip to Camp Y-Noah just over the state border, into Pennsylvania. The father-son group was there as well, and the fathers kept refilling their cups with "lemonade" and "burning sage," which was not the believable cover story they thought it was! In our group, there was a mother who had a terrible snoring problem that kept the entire cabin up, as she went to sleep at 7:00 p.m., and her snoring was so loud that no one, least of all the little ones, could sleep. Our cabin-camping trips involved rock painting, hiking, storytelling, bonding time, and trips to the candy store on the shore of Lake Erie. Ohio has such a bad reputation, but I try, at least, to find the best in everything.

Around town, we also did nation events, which I organized while I was the leader of the Y Nation. We did overnights at the zoo, Lolly the Trolley holiday activities, and even plays and musicals. It was a great way to see all the activities in your hometown, instead of travelling to someone else's. I hoped to create bonding moments with my kids and provide some good memories because I was sure their bad memories were starting to pile up too.

I was the cruise director of my children's lives. They were shuffled to baseball practice and dance-team practice. They had the matching clothes for Twins' Day during Spirit Week and the latest clothes so that they didn't suffer the bullying I had as a child. I monitored their school progress and arranged for play dates with other children. They were never short on food, never had to worry about the electricity being shut off. Clothes had to be washed and folded, and dinner needed to be served, and dishes washed. I provided them with all kinds of opportunities and material things that I didn't have as a child, but I still am not sure I did it very well at all.

The fights with David were toxic and unrelenting. I don't care that the children never had to worry about money; the environment wasn't emotionally healthy for anyone, and I'm sure it left scars. I'd like to think my efforts minimized the destruction, but that's doubtful. That's similar to expecting a soldier returning home from war to be less traumatized because on his three-day reprieves, he ate well and enjoyed a hot tub. When the memories get bad enough, the good memories are irrelevant or disappear altogether.

Every time I tried communicating with David about the one-sided nature of our relationship, I was ignored. I describe it as single-wife syndrome. I did most of the heavy lifting in the relationship. Not only did I do so without reward, but I was met with hostility, name-calling, threats to leave, and at times, things got physical. This was a nightmare. My anxiety pills and alcohol were "helping" me to calm down at the end of my fifteen-hour days, but they were just glazing over the issues at hand. I think David didn't mind the prescription abuse at first, as it made me more compliant. I was keeping my mouth shut. I was accepting my fate.

That's not a sustainable way to live. Not only could he not be bothered to help take some of the workload off my shoulders after these fifteen-hour days, but he couldn't even be bothered to listen to me vent. He was just a roommate. So I started treating him as such. If he didn't care, why did I? Why should I try to get him to treat me better instead of just walking away? Giving him more of what he already didn't appreciate would only lead to a nervous breakdown.

He had convinced me that he was the glue holding everything together. That I couldn't make it on my own. That I didn't have it in me to be a true single mother. With a home life that dysfunctional, there is no way to avoid the fact that it will begin to destroy your professional life, your mental health, your friendships, and eventually your finances. He didn't hit me, but it felt as if suicide were the only out. He was destroying my life from the inside. Disrupting everything to the point that I made more mistakes. These mistakes gave him more ammunition for the psychological abuse. It was World War III, but it was invisible abuse. Just like the Cold War with Russia, there was a real threat of imminent danger, but you couldn't prove it. There was a silent tiger waiting to pounce at just the right time. It was feeling on edge, walking on eggshells, silencing yourself to avoid fights. It was stuffing your feelings, coping in unhealthy ways. It was being mocked when you were sick, insulted after a rough day, and terrorized when all you ever wanted was peace.

If he wasn't going to provide the emotional support and physical connection I needed, I would find someone who would. I was, after all, attractive, accomplished, and blissfully unaware of my own issues that I was bringing into the relationship. I headed to the corner bar...not unaware of how long that stay would turn out to be.

Tedious Chaos

Definition:
An event that is both long and tiresome,
but also marked by chaos and confusion.

Exemplification of usage:
Him: How was your day?

Me: My ninth-period class is so wound
up that every student is just blurting out
anything and everything. It's exhausting,
and time goes by so slow. It's just tedious
chaos every day with that class!

My college years were nontraditional, to say the least. I had been married with a brand-new baby, divorced, and married again. I spent a couple of years just trying to figure out my major—I went from accounting to small business management, to elementary education. I graduated with 178 credit hours when I only needed 128. My favorite courses were geology, multimedia presentations in the classroom, and education.

My geology coursework was among the most preferred courses that I took as an undergrad at the University of Akron. Looking at the rock record is akin to looking back in time. The column of rocks that can be viewed on a cliff face tells a story. If you know how to read rocks, you can pinpoint where a flood occurred, when the sea level rose and fell, or even that a volcanic eruption took place in the not-so-distant past. I learned how the position of the tectonic plates drives the current climate, how the tilt of the Earth changes our seasons, how the moon affects evolution, and how it is essential to life on Earth. Geology reveals the big picture of the history of the Earth and is much more complete than the fossil record. Unfortunately, I learned, as a middle school teacher, not many people share my love of rocks. Geology was interesting to learn about, but it was very hard to make the subject exciting for students uninterested in rocks, which is ninety-five percent of them.

Multimedia presentation was a brand-new class when I enrolled in it as one of my electives. Little did I know how technology would take over in the coming years, but I was fortunate to have a solid foundation in multimedia when the technological revolution happened. I believe it's one of the reasons my students liked me so much; my lessons were cutting edge when enhanced with technology. I did have a knack for finding engaging and worthwhile software, as well as creating lessons that captivated the most uninterested of students. At the time, students didn't yet have technology at home, and the other teachers were still using overhead projectors. Parents began to request me as their child's eighth-grade science teacher. I was making a good impression in a very reputable district.

My multimedia project was an interdisciplinary lesson on the destruction of the rainforest. I began the lesson with the children's book *The Great Kapok Tree*, which details the plight of the rainforest. I introduced the concepts of ecosystems, plant-based medicine, and deforestation. I myself learned a volume of information about the rainforest—for example, they are essential to life on Earth as we know it—during the creation of this project. I also learned that on will take on 95% of the work to get a 95 on a project. The perfectionism of my work personality carries a huge cost; it carries the weight of gold bars at times, as I am unable to accept defeat if I find myself unsupported and unwilling to ask for help if I find myself in over my head. I've been trained not to ask for help; it's always perceived the wrong way. It either means I'm incompetent or inconvenient, but either way, it does more harm than good to ask for help.

My most enjoyable coursework as an undergrad, of course, was my education classes. I studied the stages of psychosocial development, learned the different genres of children's books, and was taught how to make bulletin boards that enhanced the classroom instruction. I learned how to teach arts and crafts, write poetry, and assess a learning disability. The education coursework was comprehensive, to say the least, but only prepared me for about five percent of what it takes to be a classroom teacher. It didn't prepare me for the reality of discipline problems, getting along with changing bosses, or dealing with difficult parents who are convinced that their child could do no wrong. The vast majority of my teaching was on-the-job learning; public education's policies changed yearly, which made it difficult to truly master anything. As soon as I really had a handle on any new program, the district or state government threw the baby out with the bathwater, and we had to start from scratch at the beginning of the new year.

I eventually combined all three of my favorite classes into exemplary lessons in the classroom. I wanted to turn my love of learning into a career, and I did this successfully. Most of my students treated me like royalty, showering me with praise and attention. My professors were dedicated professionals who probably weren't paid enough, but I am indebted to them for life, as they provided me a roadmap for both my career and my life. I most certainly would not change a thing.

It was the early nineties, and the United States was changing. The grunge music scene had taken over. Bill Clinton had recently been elected our president after twelve years of Republican leadership, and the dot-com industry was exploding. The economy was growing, and inflation was low. It was the beginning of my career; I was ambitious, motivated, loved by the students, and the new star employee. Technology was new, and students, by and large, didn't have it at home. I was teaching in an affluent district that had access to technology, so I was able to introduce many interesting lessons and provide some relatability by using the new technology.

But the end of my career, I considered teaching to be a type of tedious chaos. My days were both long and tiresome, but also marked by chaos and confusion. I taught approximately 180 students per day—some special needs, some gifted, and many in between. It's impossible for one person to serve all the needs of 180 students in a day; unfortunately, not all my students got the best of me. I became the victim of my own success; I was overloaded with work as I was the top-performing science teacher. As I had never learned to stand up for myself—and held the misguided belief that good employees don't ruffle feathers—this only made the situation worse.

I taught eighth-grade science. Most people thought I must be crazy to like eighth grade, but I loved it. In high school, students really have a chip on their shoulders; in elementary school, students can't be reasoned with. So eighth grade was perfect for me. The students at that age still respected authority and had enough brain development to study some of the harder stuff.

The basics taught in first and second grade seem to be the hardest. If I'm trying to teach you to read, and you don't understand the word "the," I'm at a loss as to how to explain the word "the." I knew my limitations as a teacher, and the middle ground of eighth grade was perfect for me. Not too advanced, not too basic, but just right. The biggest problem with teaching middle school is that the staff often are about as immature as the students. You would think teachers would be above pettiness, gossip, and revenge, but that couldn't be further from the truth. Some teachers there made it their job to bring down their colleagues. Me, I was too busy grading papers and developing lessons to be concerned about my colleagues, but that's just who I am.

There were so many funny moments in the classroom and so many lively personalities. Of course, some students were afraid of their own shadow, some were quirky, and some were disgruntled, but that's what made the classroom fun—the mix of personalities. Seeing the class clown cheer up the disgruntled, seeing the quirky nerd befriend the loner. Those moments in the classroom made it all worthwhile.

I also put my foot in my mouth more often than I would like to admit. I once had a principal ask me how things were going, and I responded, "Busier than a—" I abruptly stopped because I had almost said, "Busier than a one-legged man in an ass-kicking contest," but this man had only one leg. So after stopping myself, I simply said, "Busier than a bee." What a near miss.

There was also a time when I had a very memorable student named Lance. Lance was the kind of kid who hit puberty in fifth grade. He and his friends joked that he received a shaving kit for Christmas in sixth grade. We were tie-dyeing T-shirts in the classroom, randomly knotting the shirts, only to find what pattern may emerge after they'd been through the wash cycle. Lo and behold, Lance's shirt had swirls and other patterns in just the right places; they made it look like an anatomically correct diagram of the human body. Swirls right where his chest would be, ripples looked like a six-pack on his abs, and, of course, a protrusion coming up from down below, at the bottom of his shirt. It was a one-in-a-million occurrence. It could not have looked more like the diagram of a human body if we had tried. Of course, we didn't know this until he tried the shirt on for the class, only for the class to erupt in laughter. He was a confident student; an awkward student might've been embarrassed, but Lance rolled with the punches, which made it even funnier.

But nothing could be more embarrassing than the day I told my class to call me Tea Bag. It was the day that Dimebag Darrell from Pantera was killed onstage, and the students, quite upset, filed into my room. As we talked about the news story, I tried to calm them down and redirect their attention to class. I did this by saying, "I always wanted a nickname. I drink a lot of tea. Why don't you call me Tea Bag!" The class hit the floor like sacks of flour; they hit the floor so fast. The laughter was uncontrollable. I, naïve as I was, had no idea I had just told my students to call me the name of a sex act. I don't know if I regained control of the class that day, but in teaching, you'll have that sometimes.

Perhaps my best day of teaching was a day that there was no teaching at all. It was our field day, and the school was divided into red, white, and blue teams. We had games and competitions all day long, and at the end of the day, the white team and the red team were tied. It was determined that two teachers would play cornhole to break the tie.

I was representing the red team, and a man named Tony, who happened to be my nemesis, was representing the white team. Tony was a truly awful person. He was later fired for sexual harassment as he routinely destroyed the lives of the female employees at the middle school, and it was he whom I was up against for the tie-breaking game. I had never played cornhole before, and he was a seasoned coach.

Against all odds, I beat Tony in cornhole, onstage, at the eleventh hour in front of over one thousand students. I was in complete shock. I had never even played before! My students were cheering and chanting my name, and I was presented with a trophy that was about three feet tall for winning the game. But it wasn't until I left school that day that I realized how much my students loved me. The fact that I, a five-foot-four, petite woman beat Tony in full view of over a thousand people was pretty sweet too. He did, after all, terrorize my work bestie for a year when she wouldn't sleep with him. It just sent the message that I would always win the long game.

After school, I got in my Honda SUV and immediately got stopped in traffic right out of the parking lot. Throngs of students were everywhere. It being field day, everyone was walking to the ice-cream store after school, not getting picked up by parents or taking the bus. The students, still overjoyed that I'd won Team Day over Tony, started grabbing dandelions and placing them on the hood of my car as I was stuck in traffic. I felt like LeBron James after winning a championship. Students chanted they loved me and threw flowers on my car. It was a level of fandom that I had never experienced before.

Those are the days that make me miss teaching, but the reality is that day-to-day teaching is not like that. Day-to-day, you have 180 papers to grade, parent-teacher conferences at 7:00 a.m. in the morning, and money shortages that lead to decisions between toilet paper and copy paper. And then, of course, there's the usual office politics.

There is Policy Pete, who patrols the halls to make sure no one is violating the dress code—he was monitoring the teachers, not the students. The students started looking as if they were hitting the club after school as the leadership at the school declined. Look, I'm supposed to be a respected professional, and the job is running me into the ground. If I wear jeans on the wrong day because I'm confused as to what day Dress-Down Day is, the last thing I need is Policy Pete reporting me to Administration. Administration is to blame, too, for encouraging the behavior of a playground bully like Policy Pete. Didn't Pete have *actual* work to do?

Then there's always Part-Time Paulie, the employee who misses at least one day a week of work, but never seems to get flack for being a shitty employee. Part-Time Paulie does the bare minimum, year in and year out, collects his pension, and generally gives the profession a bad name. He typically stays close friends with Policy Pete just to stay out of trouble. It's best to keep your friends close, but your enemies even closer.

As I said, the teachers themselves were acting like middle school students. The treatment of public school teachers was getting worse by the day. Depending on which talking head you listened to on the news, we were the reason why the economy was strained, why the new generation didn't have a work ethic, and why we were behind the rest of the world in innovative technology; the reporters completely ignored that we had zero control over what was happening. Men in suits in ivory towers were making decisions without ever considering the ramifications. But, yes, the math teacher, who tutors without extra pay, is the evil that has befallen our society. The whole system was broken, and I was in the middle of it.

But I became so good at what I did that I was made the department head in charge of all the supplies, mixing the chemicals, and staying on top of new training. I mentored new employees and developed an honors-program curriculum. I was so proud of myself for being the favorite teacher among the students. And I was the favorite for the right reasons. My lessons were engaging. My test scores were on point. I was at the top of my game.

So Little Oppenheimer did what narcissists like to do when they feel threatened or intimidated—they turn up the heat on the mind games and threats at home. The threats to leave grew more frequent, my drinking grew heavier, and the kids just tried to stay away.

Finally, during a fight in which Little O threatened to leave, I said, "Go—I'm not going to stop you anymore. You've wanted to leave for a while. This isn't working, and truly we should've pulled the plug years ago."

He left, but I didn't realize at the time, that he wasn't going to go away quietly. I had the nerve to call his bluff, and he wasn't going to be embarrassed by it. I couldn't wait to be free, and I had bigger problems than trying to please this unpleasable man-child. It was abundantly clear by this point that nothing I did was ever going to make him happy. I could make more money, I could buy him a fancy car, I could do everything right, but he was determined to be unhappy.

My escalating drinking surely wasn't helping, but he failed to realize the abuse was exacerbating the problem. He failed to realize that shaming me for trying to keep my mental health in check was only hurting both of us. The relationship had gone south, had turned into a conveyor belt of pain and pointlessness. There was no affection, only insults. There was no gratitude, only disappointed looks indicating I didn't measure up to what he wanted.

I had bigger problems than trying to put a smile on a narc's face; my mother had recently been diagnosed with cancer. She was five or six years sober at this time, but she developed cancer of the esophagus, not unusual for a drinker. Vodka is hard on the throat.

Stress was escalating from all sides. I was feeling the squeeze of raising my children while feeling like a single wife. Public education was getting more stressful by the day; my mother's health was hanging in the balance. Mommy wine culture had now taken over to minimize and normalize my issues. It was a recipe for disaster. But at least, now, with my husband gone, I could come home and sleep in peace. I didn't realize then that Little Oppenheimer would never be capable of peace.

Bi-Spectrum

Definition:
*What you are when one parent is bipolar,
and the other is on the autism spectrum.*

Exemplification of Usage:
*Him: You know, you're very unusual. You
have such a creative flair, but you're also
very scientific.*

Me: Thank you, it's the bi-spectrum.

August 11, 2009
I burst into my mother's hospital room. She has no voice
box at this point; it was removed after stage 4 cancer was
found in her esophagus. Even though she has no voice,
I've learned to read lips to communicate with her. We talk
for hours on end, even though she makes no noise. These
end days are precious, but today I'm entirely self-absorbed
and only thinking of myself. I rush in to tell her how much
my life sucks.

As I sit with this mood, my mother lies dying, and I apparently have no comprehension how much emotional turmoil she must be going through. I launch into a diatribe about my relationship woes, financial woes, and career gaffes. At this point, I'm not yet at the age where I can see the big picture. Again, I'm only thinking of myself, and I will not realize for a decade how much her death will affect me. I'm her medical power of attorney, so I will determine when she gets disconnected.

As I said, I won't realize until later that this is my last conversation that I will ever have with my mother; I'm sweating the small stuff, and at the end of your life, you'll realize it's almost all small stuff. I could've talked about so many things, but I didn't. I made the day about me—which is necessary at times—but this was the wrong day and the wrong time.

Where to even begin with my mother? Well, at the beginning, I suppose.

I was born in September of 1970 in a town called Montague, Massachusetts. My father was a professor of radio astronomy at UMass in Amherst. They purchased the house in Amherst in 1968 or thereabouts, leaving Cleveland behind for a time.

I loved Amherst, but I have no memories of ever living there; my memories were from the visits to see my father. My first actual memory is yelling to my brother, "There goes Massachusetts!" while in the wayback of the family's Travelall. My first memory of Massachusetts is from 1975, when as a kindergartner, my mother put my brother and me on a plane to be chaperoned by the airline staff. I remember returning to "my old house" and looking at it for the first time, confused that my brother remembered the house, but I didn't. The kids in the neighborhood, were all excited that I was back, and I didn't remember them at all. This was a sign that I suffered from emotional blackouts but didn't realize it. Trauma often hides in these blackouts.

The house in Massachusetts was a Dutch Colonial in a suburban housing development. It had old cars out front that were on a to-do list to get restored "one day." It was an exceptionally large house, especially for the time—four bedrooms, a walk-out basement, and a yard wooded with fir trees. It was a gem of a house that had not yet begun to look dilapidated.

My family of six—two older brothers, one twin brother, my parents, and I—lived there until 1974. My parents were very different from the parents of the time. They were liberal politically, and champions for social justice and change; they came of age in the 1960s. I'm pretty sure my father was on the autism spectrum, but nobody even knew that diagnosis existed at that time. My mother was bipolar, which was even more misunderstood then. This makes me bi-spectrum, as my friend Karen would say. I'm bipolar and on the autism spectrum. It makes life interesting, to say the least. To say that it causes social and communication problems, is an understatement.

But in 2009, my mother was dying from a lifetime of bad choices. She'd smoked cigarettes her whole life—the general attitude on cigarettes was so different during the 1900s. You were cool and provocative if you smoked, unlike being guilty of the dirty habit it is perceived as now. By the age of four, my mother had me lighting her cigarettes for her. Before you think ill of her, everyone was doing it. Mob mentality is a powerful thing. Drunk driving was not even considered a bad thing at this time. If you got caught driving drunk in the seventies, there was a good chance the cop would even drive you home.

When I was born, my father filmed my birth. It's the greatest gift the universe has ever given me. Even though the home movie has no sound, I can now read lips, so I know the first words my mother ever told me. Being one of a pair of twins during a time when ultrasound technology was not even a thing, I was born premature and at a weight of less than six pounds. I was jaundiced and put into an incubator that looked like a microwave. I saw this home movie many times when I was growing up. I did not realize the significance of it until the day of my mother's funeral.

I disconnected her from the life-support machines in October of 2009; I know the last words she ever said. From the home movie, I know the first words she ever said to me—truly a gift from the universe. I can write all this now with the perspective of a saint, but it took thirteen years, a divorce, empty nesting, four rock bottoms, and eventual sobriety to get here.

The emotional toll of having to make this end-of-life decision, of watching her die over the course of six months, and of David berating me the whole time that I was neglecting my household responsibilities most definitely forced me to cross the line into addiction. It was affecting every part of my life. I was so angry, though. I felt society was broken. How was one woman supposed to handle what I was being asked to handle? Juggling a full-time job that was being demonized by politicians; raising three children and trying to do a better job than my parents; trying to please an unpleasant man; trying, until the bitter end, to comfort my mother, who was on her way out of this world; and listening until the death rattle went silent?

Not surprisingly, when I crossed that line into addiction, David left. The tiger pounced when I was at my weakest, when I needed him the most. He had to make sure I was a broken shell of a woman before he would leave me, the woman he had wanted a divorce from since day four, alone. My support system was nonexistent, as my older daughter had left for college. I lost my teaching job over "conduct unbecoming the profession"—high number of absences, falling behind on deadlines, students accusing me of some ridiculous crap they claimed happened. For instance, they claimed I taught them how to make crystal meth in the classroom. But some of the information was true enough that I lost my job. It was my first rock bottom, although I didn't recognize it as such. At the time, I didn't realize how bad I would let things get before I finally surrendered. But, right now, I'm just trying to hold it all together while carrying the weight of the world on my shoulders, a world that is getting ripped apart and pulled in different directions daily.

Time to Get on the Ferry

Definition:
A common expression on the northern coast of Ohio, where tourists binge drinks on the islands until it's time to get on the ferry to travel to the mainland and sober up.

Exemplification of usage:
Me: I've been day drinking all weekend.

Him: It's time to get on the ferry!

Right before the real estate crash of 2009, my married life was going well, my kids were growing up, and I was at the height of my professional success as a science teacher. I was responsible for developing an honors program at school, and it was incredibly successful. My students were thriving; I was thriving. When your professional life is going well, it's easy for things to fall into place at home.

Facing an empty nest in a few short years, I thought that surely there would be extra money to be found after bills were paid. David and I decided to purchase a vacation condo on the northern shore of Ohio. The condo was close to the Lake Erie Islands—an island chain I would later refer to as the poor man's resort. It was small, but with this place, you paid for the view. Right on the beaches of Lake Erie, it was incredible to wake up and look right out onto the water in the morning. It wasn't the ocean, but it was close. A nobility you can't find in the city. A tranquility you can't find in the suburbs. A view you can't find in the country. It was perfect, if small. A peaceful and serene weekend getaway just an hour and a half from home.

The problem was, David never liked the vacation condo. This wasn't mentioned until after the divorce papers were signed. He never had a problem with any-thing until after the papers were signed, much like our marriage. David even accused me of buying the vacation condo to impress my dad. I was shocked—what would even prompt this accusation? David was clearly threat-ened by my professional success, as he wasn't having any. The only way he could strike back was to criticize me into an image problem.

The condo became a place for my kids and me to blow off steam. An in-ground pool, a local marina, and plenty of eateries gave the place a resort feel. It was spectac-ular. But, soon enough, the market crashed, work stress increased, and David and I separated for a time.

During the separation, the condo was a place for my friends and me to hang out and befriend locals. Trying to get the feel of this locale became a part-time party for Patty, Joy, and me. We ventured onto the islands for the night, taking the ferry to and from. Once on the island, party mode was in full swing. Shots, shopping, and live music! On the islands, you didn't even drive cars; you just rented golf carts to tool around barhopping and dodging piles of puke from novice binge drinkers. Patty and Joy fought like cats and dogs; they were too much alike to get along. They went for the same type of guys, took too long getting ready, and looked like fluff chicks. Tequila made their clothes come off far too easily, and neither ever said no to nose candy. It was a summer of numbing at the expense of our livers, all palaver about plans that never materialized, and acting like anything but ladies. I was still living with the ghost of David and running from many ghosts within myself.

The latest holiday to be celebrated by binge drinking on the island was Christmas in July. Torrential downpours marked the occasion, but we still set out to party. By morning, we needed more than a few Tylenols and a Gatorade. At least, we didn't need a lawyer. I always thought I was smarter than the average bear, but not smart enough to stay out of trouble, evidently. Not smart enough to stop swallowing an entire paycheck in a weekend. Not smart enough to hold on to my dignity.

The duality of my nature was increasing. I was a walking contradiction. My divided selves were growing further apart. Trying to be all things to all people was tearing me apart. My separate selves were trapped just as the circus clowns are while waiting to get out of the small Volkswagen. The singular Susan felt more unattainable by the minute.

To take my mind off my mounting problems, Joy, Patty, and I headed out for a night of drinking and possible debauchery. Would we spend our money on clothes we would never wear? Or would we wake up next to guys whose names we wouldn't remember come morning? The possibilities were endless.

As the night progressed, Joy and Patty had their eyes on the same guy. An island full of mediocre men, and they must pick the same one with whom to do nine-inch curls. The conversation got heated, and it became obvious they were heading toward a cat fight. I'm the only one of us who was wondering why they were fighting over a guy they'd only known for five minutes. Apparently, someone forgot to call dibs.

I had no interest in hooking up with any stranger, so I just sat nursing a drink and letting the drama unfold. Within minutes, all hell broke loose, and we were kicked out of the bar. Jaime yelled at me to take sides, which left me confused as I didn't know what the hell was going on. I felt as if I'd walked into the last fifteen minutes of a movie. Jaime, furious that I didn't take her side, stormed off in one direction, Paula in another. I found myself alone on the island and mysteriously got blackout drunk. I only had two drinks—wink, wink. Not sure how I got drunk.

I suddenly realized that I was stranded on the island for the night. I'd missed the last ferry off the island, and there were no rooms for rent. The island was packed solid for the summer. Like the Virgin Mary, I am out in the cold, sleeping on the sidewalk. See? I am smarter than the average bear. Wink, wink, not really.

As I sat gobbling a slice of pizza from the nearest food shack, an island local tells me I can couch surf that night instead of sleeping on the cement. Unsure of what his real intentions were, I followed him back to his apartment. To my horror, he doesn't want to sleep with me. Are you kidding me right now? I'm a catch you just scooped off the pavement, a catch who was gobbling pepperoni pizza at 3:00 a.m. But, apparently, he had standards. Just my luck.

In the morning, I headed back to the condo while wondering what became of Paula and Jaime. I had my own problems to deal with and decided I would figure it out when I got back to the mainland. I needed to charge my phone, scrub my teeth, and freshen up after a night with the sexless innkeeper. It was definitely time to get off the ferry and onto the mainland.

Joy and Patty didn't arrive home until 4:00 p.m. They apparently found a different mediocre man to fight over;

then they decided there were enough men for everyone and made up. Morning light was the time to realize that they were fighting over an average, ugly guy with no job. A solid two if there ever was one.

As the notches, blackouts, and hangovers increased for all three of us, I was beginning to wonder if I should get on the ferry for good.

An Easter Bunny, some Hose Lickers, and a Karen

Definition of Easter Bunny:
Superficial, shallow women who seem so enticing at first. Upon further inspection, they are found to be as hollow as a chocolate Easter bunny.

Exemplification of Usage:
Me: She's so beautiful, but couldn't be more shallow if you tried. She's like an Easter bunny.

David and I separated shortly after the economic downturn of 2009. My mother had passed in that year, I was newly single, and my oldest had just left for college. My entire support system collapsed inside of three months. All three had provided help and support I had yet to recognize. Naturally, I took this opportunity to live the party side of college years I had never experienced. I had become a mother at nineteen, and although I had earned both a bachelor's and a master's degree, I never had any college fun. My relationships with my drinking buddies were firmly solidified, while the friendships with successful, productive, or goal-oriented people withered on the vine as my priorities continued to revert to the same ones I had in my teenage years. I felt I had missed out on life while always taking care of children, my mother, or either of my husbands. Now was my time to live!

I quickly became a staple at the local pub, became best friends with a girl I gave a ride home, and made another friend at a local fundraiser. With two new drinking friends, a condo on the lake, and feeling untethered, I was expecting nothing but good things to happen. Unfortunately, some of the women I befriended had questionable morals and otherwise sketchy decision-making skills. I lacked assertiveness, was still firmly in people-pleasing mode, and just went with the flow even if it was to my detriment. I became oblivious to the fact that I still had a demanding job, a house to maintain, and my youngest was in middle school and needed the same guidance I lacked as a child. I was perpetuating every possible dysfunction and was the last to know. The fun I was chasing superseded everything, even at the expense of my family, my bills, and my own welfare. But FOMO, right? My philosophy was "You only live once. I deserve this time. This will be fulfilling."

Jen, the woman I gave a ride home, quickly became my best friend. She was also single and had never had children. She was the life of the party—just what I was looking for. One night, she and I headed to the local plaza of sin—the plaza in town that had a bar, a divorce lawyer, a liquor store, and a tattoo parlor. A strip joint, a porn shop, and a casino were just across the street. As we sat downing shots, she decided to sell me on the idea of getting a tattoo. She then took me on a quick tour of her tattoos. She had a stained-glass heart on her foot, commemorating her hobby of creating stained glass pieces, a divorce tattoo, and one representing her love of dogs. Tattoos were just becoming more mainstream then, and I had several coworkers who had them. After a flimsy sales pitch, I decided to get the tattoo, my impulsivity on full display once again.

Jen, Kim, and I headed to that tattoo parlor. I had no idea how expensive they were. I also had no idea how much pain I was going to be in. We strolled around the lobby, looking at the artwork, while the very emo employees stood close by. It was Friday evening, and I'm sure they didn't want last-minute customers. We had a pretty good buzz from the shots at the bar, so I thought I would be all right with the pain. I decided to get a lithium molecule in my bikini area. The molecule represented my job as a science teacher, as well as my bipolar struggles. It was no larger than a half-dollar, and I was told it cost ninety-five dollars. At which point, Kim jumped up and said she had a volleyball game to go to that she'd forgotten about, and

Jen decided she didn't have the money. They were both bailing on me!

Jen, to exert some damage control, gave me a couple of pills to relax. I took them, not caring about the consequences of mixing them with hard liquor. Soon enough, I was far past tipsy, which should have caused the employee to kick me out, but they took my money anyway. It was painful and expensive enough that I wouldn't do it again, but somehow that tattoo felt like a rite of passage.

Not too long after that, Jen decided to give twelve-step programs a try. She had lost her job due to the economic downturn, and her escalating financial difficulties and pressure from family forced her into the rooms of recovery. I attended many meetings with her, we took many hikes in the park, and we even discussed freelance writing during the year we were best friends. That year really laid the foundation for where I am today, but, of course, I didn't know this at the time. Her sobriety and my escalating addiction came between us. As my addiction escalated, work problems, money problems, and child-rearing problems began multiplying. But rather than address those problems, I decided to find a new best friend.

Karen, from the fundraiser was next up. Karen and I met quite serendipitously at a local fundraiser for a mutual friend, and we connected immediately. I had an opening for a bestie, and her philosophy on life was that it is too short to be boring. She was recently single, living with her sister, and shared my love of craft beer. My craft-beer "hobby" was a snobby disguise for my drinking problem, but she didn't know it yet.

She invited me to celebrate Cleveland Beer Week with her. We drank on a train, on a boat, and at the fair. We drank from East Fourth to West Sixth, to the parking lots before the Browns' games. We drank at networking events, hipster bars, but never at my house. Life was too short to be boring. She tired of me quite quickly.

My habit of overconsumption started causing problems almost immediately. One crisp fall day, we decided to tail-gate before the Browns' game. At the muni lot, we began drinking by 8:00 a.m. Shots of apple pie were on deck— I always found apple pie dangerously tasty. It went down like fruit punch on a hot day. There were games set up in the lot—cornhole and a large-size Jenga set—and grills for food. I was too preoccupied with drinking to be concerned with food. The hard liquor in the apple pie, early in the morning, and lack of food quickly turned the day side-ways. I began vomiting and passed out inside the stadium about two minutes into the game. Karen had to drag me back to her sister's and tuck me in by two in the afternoon.

Other times, she became worried that it was unsafe for me to drive, so she asked me to stop drinking and have some water before heading home. Once, we were celebrating Pi Day at a trendy new bar, and I had taken too many pills before heading there. I was as glazed as a morning doughnut before even arriving. Karen was not happy. The impunity with which I was operating a car in a clearly unsafe condition was alarming, to say the least.

By the fall of that year, David and I were trying to reconcile again, and she invited us to the casino. Karen was much more of a night owl than I, and we didn't even arrive at the casino until around eleven. I practically chugged my drinks and got irrationally annoyed with everyone. When the waitress wouldn't serve drinks fast enough, I stormed out of the casino, having decided to walk home in the middle of the night in late October. I hadn't realized that home was five miles away.

About a mile into the trip, I realized that I had bitten off more than I could chew. I was very close to my friend Sarah's house. It was one thirty in the morning. I was drunk, cold, and tired, so why not see if I could sleep there? Unbelievably, she answered the door and let me in. I thought I just crashed on the couch in relief. But, the next day, Sarah recounted that when I used the bathroom, I broke the toilet somehow, and when I lit a cigarette on the stove, I fell back to sleep without turning the stove off. She was quite pissed. Why shouldn't she be?

My world, and the way I viewed it, was getting more myopic by the minute. I was in damage-control mode, but I was still creating more damage by the day, trying to avoid all the pain I was in, and only causing more pain to everyone around me. I wanted an apology from David for all the ways he had hurt me. I wanted apologies from my parents for not ever providing emotional support and good relationship role models. I wanted apologies from past employers who had let me go. I wanted apologies for my traumas, but no one thought that they had done anything wrong. And I, conditioned into silence, never spoke up until much too late. And in the process, I was traumatizing people, like my daughters, who had done nothing wrong. Generational shit was rolling downhill and picking up speed with time.

Corporate Serfdom

Definition:
Modern-day serfdom in the workforce—the mistreatment of employees by paying low wages and providing no health care. Typically, there is a toxic manager who focuses on what you do wrong, even minimally; never focuses on what you do well; and never understands that you have a life outside of work. Often, there is a demerit-point system for attendance—for instance, earning one point for calling in sick, even if you are a single mother with sick children. After earning a certain number of points, you could face loss of pay or even termination. Corporate slavery has risen dramatically due to the decline of unions and the right-to-work laws.

Exemplification of usage:
Me: Kathy just called in sick today because, when she woke up, her fiancé next to her was dead in bed.

Krystal: Can you believe Sheri's response to Kathy? Since it was an unplanned absence, Kathy will earn a point! Then, the boss told her she wouldn't get paid for her bereavement time because he was just a fiancé, not yet a husband.

Me: So wait! Are you telling me that Kathy won't receive the paid bereavement because he was "just" a fiancé? I can't believe Sheri would even mention points! Like Kathy gives a shit right now.

Krystal: This is corporate serfdom. Remember when the computers were nonfunctional, and we had to show up to this damn cube farm all three days and just sit at a nonworking computer?

Me: That was horribly boring! Right? Right! This is just a form of modern-day feudalism. I hate it here. I get no time off during the day to be able to interview. It is almost impossible to get your time off approved!

In 2009 the economy crashed and along with it the real estate market. Americans tend to spend more than they earn, and this came back to haunt many people. They lost their jobs, their family, and their homes. I was soon to be in that category but didn't know it yet.

In March 2012, I lost my teaching job. Since my self-esteem could fit in a thimble at the time, I didn't do well at the interviews I managed to obtain. I ended up at a cube farm for a property-preservation company. It was a call center that dealt with foreclosed properties from the economic crisis of 2009. The job felt as abusive as a toxic relationship. Emails were monitored. It was a dead-end job with no escape. The boss that I had at that time was a ruthless bitch, to put it bluntly. She quite literally lived and died for work. Even when she had breast cancer, she didn't miss work. Even during chemotherapy, she didn't miss work, which is an exceptionally bad idea; your immune system is quite compromised during chemotherapy. I will tell you what I have told everybody in my life—on your deathbed, you will not ever say, "I wish I had worked more! If only my emails were organized!"

On that job, I learned the importance of overgrown grass! Irate neighbors of the foreclosed properties called to scream about the tall grass next door They complained for half an hour about the uncut grass. It was my job to call the landscape vendor and arrange for the grass to be cut. I was exceptionally good at what I did, not that I received any praise. If anything, I was a victim of what is called the Peter Principle. I was promoted to my own level of incompetence.

As I said, my boss was a bitch. She started emails with "Please help me understand…" That phrase rubbed me the wrong way; it felt as rough to my psyche as rubbing the fur on a cat backwards. I became irate almost instantly when I received her emails. Further aggravating the problem was that the issue in question was usually a clusterfuck created by someone else. I was handed a disaster, and then, somehow, it turned into my fault.

I was hated by the other incompetent people at work. On any given day, I made 90 phone calls to vendors to get overdue work orders done. My coworkers shoe shopped online and then became angry when I outperformed them. As I said, it felt as toxic as an abusive domestic relationship. Why I worried about that job at night—which, by the way, paid thirteen dollars an hour while I had a master's degree going to waste—I have no idea. I wasn't taking my own advice about minimizing the impact of work on my life.

I was there for four full years. In 2016, they lost a huge account with a large bank in seventeen states. This led to a drastic workforce reduction. By that time, I had been promoted to team leader—a dead-end, boring data-entry position. We weren't allowed to talk to our coworkers, even during our downtime or a full blackout. This position made us stare at our computers in silence, as if we were petulant children who had been punished for being too loud during mom's afternoon siesta.

I started drinking as soon as I got off work. I passed out by 8:00 p.m. and then awoke at around two or three with extreme anxiety that I didn't realize was caused by the drinking. David was back in my life for a minute, until he realized how much my disease had progressed. My overall health was in complete shambles. My skin was red and puffy; I had heart palpitations, diarrhea, poor nutrition, and was the heaviest I had ever been in my life. I weighed more than I did when nine months pregnant.

When I was fired from that job for incompetence, David started official divorce proceedings. He was already seeing someone new. He said it was because I ruined his retirement. He didn't seem to care that he was fully culpable for my destruction from the inside. My issues with alcohol began early in life, but his cruelty, neglect, and psychological abuse did not help matters at all. And yet, I still wasn't done drinking.

Counter Creeper

Definition:
That one guy or girl who is always sitting at the counter at your local bar or diner.

Exemplification of Usage:
Me: So, that dude Jim asked me out.

Him: He asks everyone out. He's a counter creeper.

It had been over a year since the divorce proceedings were started, and there was still no end in sight. Working eleven-hour days at the time, and still drinking, I stopped at the bar every night on my home for dinner and drinks. As I sat alone at the bar, inevitably, it ended up with one person asking another person out on a date. This was a local bar that was very family friendly; I did feel safe going in there by myself. I became a counter creeper.

I inevitably ended up talking to the single guys at the bar. These were not the type of guys, though, that were actual boyfriend material, but I wasn't girlfriend material either. One guy took me on a date to Whiskey Island and then decided, halfway through the date, he'd rather be with Paula. I went on a few dates with another guy who happened to have a stuttering problem, but he eventually stopped seeing me because he found someone. Then there was Frank.

I was working at a nonprofit that helped students get their GEDs. It was on Kinsman in Cleveland. It was in the absolute worst part of town, but that opportunity changed my life. Anyhow, one night I went to the bar, and it was election night—not THE election night, but still an election. I believe the blue wave came through that year. The place was packed.

I managed to score a seat by the lift-up bar, the one separated by a space and used by staff to come and go. Frank was leaning against the wall close by, and he started talking to me. I happened to bring up the TV show *Vikings* and proceeded to start an intellectual conversation about the Vikings storming Paris. You know, bar talk. Had I known he was straight-up obsessed with the Vikings, I would've realized what would unfold next—literally obsessed with me. *Vikings* was his favorite TV show.

I ran out of money and didn't have my ATM card, so I announced I was leaving, and he offered money so I could stay. I borrowed twenty bucks and told him I'd give it back to him the next day. The next day arrived, and I left work three hours early to get to the bar to see Frank. He asked me to be his girlfriend that night—we hadn't even had a proper date yet—and three days later he told me that he was in love with me. That escalated quickly! I really did enjoy my time with Frank at first, but I was manic and drinking, and mania can physically change you and distort reality. I was in no frame of mind to be starting a relationship.

My aunt made the comment once that she resented bipolarity being considered a mental illness because it causes your whole physiology to change. Your eyes sparkle, your skin glows, and you feel as if you were fifteen years old again. Your metabolism is ridiculously fast, so you don't wake up drunk; in fact, you don't have hangovers even after you've had fifteen beers. You do suffer headaches and sleep disturbances, to put it mildly. Your energy levels are insane. The creative part of your brain unlocks.

I lost weight, developed muscles out of nowhere when manic, and started blogging. I was living the Alice in Wonderland quote about having "six impossible ideas before breakfast." I felt fantastic.

As my marriage ended—the last two years were miserable—I was in a manic depression. I've only had two manic-depression episodes in my life, and debilitating doesn't quite describe it. No sex drive, weight gain, difficulty with almost everything, and on top of that, I was drinking during the depressive episodes. But manic episodes can be just as damaging; spending money, shopping, indulging in sex and substances—that's all you want when you're manic. Besides, you're going to be a millionaire by next week, so don't worry about draining your 401(k). Your confidence is so exaggerated that you feel as if you'll be the thing everyone in Hollywood is talking about by next week.

Frank and I didn't even wait a week before the relationship got physical. He was living with his dad, so in probably less than two weeks, Frank moved in with me. I was in the middle of a relapse, and I was manic! Things would go to holy hell by the time summer came.

Frank was a golfer, a bird-watcher, and a reader of books, so he said. I thought he was the smartest guy I'd ever met. He had made four holes in one during his life and could identify any bird that we came across during our trips to the park. When our conversations were about historical events, he seemed well-versed in whatever subject—telling me the reasons we lost the Vietnam War, for instance. And, by the way, whatever I thought on the subject was wrong; my brain had been poisoned by propaganda.

He was also an alcoholic in denial. Here's how this plays out: he can drink the way he wants to, but I can drink the way I want to, thank God. Someone who thinks there is no problem with my drinking. I hit the jackpot! No rules on my drinking! We would be doing shots until the wee hours of the morning. He'd barely be able to get out bed in the morning. That was no deterrent for doing it again, however. I, on the other hand, woke up feeling as if not even an ounce of alcohol had entered my body. He could skip days of drinking if too hungover, unlike me. This gave me the illusion that he was a social drinker, or, at worst, a gray-area drinker.

One night, I took my nighttime medication along with the alcohol. I could barely speak. After that, Frank convinced me to go off the pills. Everybody told me I wasn't bipolar, but that's because the *medication was working*. I abruptly stopped all medication on the advice of a guy I barely knew, a guy who had no clue what he was talking about in terms of psychiatric medication.

A few weeks out, my brain was more active than ever. The impossible ideas just kept coming and coming. I couldn't blog fast enough. I was going to be an Internet sensation. I had ideas for a whole empire of blogging with merchandise, the works. Houston, we have lift off! Many chronically manic—hypomanic—people come off as type A personalities with ambition and drive, and, really, they are during an episode. As the episodes are unsustainable and require medical intervention, the ideas don't go anywhere.

I got increasingly aggravated with my job. My boss obviously hated me because I was smarter, prettier, and more likable. I quit my job. I was living in my childhood home, which was occupied by Mother until her death. My father lived there for a time, and he was a hoarder. I couldn't stop cleaning, cooking, developing get-rich-quick schemes. I started my own dictionary, the dictionary on which this book is based. Getting the house together, I was up at 2:00 a.m., hammering nails into the walls for my many decorations. Twelve-step material was all over the bedroom.

I eventually told Frank that I had been to rehab and a halfway house, with no results. He said there was nothing wrong with my drinking and not to worry about a thing. He thought my drinking habits were normal. That was the best news I'd ever heard. I told him I thought we should get married.

What follows are journal entries from that time period.

January 2018

> *My fiancé and I have some 1950s habits at our home. I now stay at home and make money from my side hustles.*

Side hustles—I don't recall any side hustles. They existed only in my mind. I was blogging like crazy, convinced I was going to be the next Jenna Marbles.

> *I do the majority of the housework—he works two jobs. It's been wonderful—I write new recipes every day and make lunch and dinner (but I need*

to hire a dishwasher lol). He does some housework too. He is very chivalrous too.

On Sundays, at first, we apparently started a tradition, new to us, that I really enjoyed. We took a Sunday drive through the metro parks. The parkway is long and winding; the snow has created a winter wonderland. He points out hawks in the sky. I announce what hikes I have done. The conversation dissipates rapidly as we just absorb the beauty of the trees. We do this the next day too. It will be a habit for a minute. We can enjoy this season from the comfort of our car. Although the blizzard snow is fresh, the roads have been plowed and are safe.

As I sit here thinking about those drives and all the pleasant memories I have created in a short period of time, more pleasant memories than in the last five years with David. Sometimes we sit on the couch or at the table in the kitchen without technology in this Norman Rockwell setting. There is no TV on in the distance. The cell phone is being ignored. The kitchen provides a fantastic view—the squirrels are looking for food—well, we'll obviously fix that. Silence returns until I show him my squirrel meme. Or, no, it's crows. We sincerely have a youthful sense of humor. It keeps the relationship interesting. No trauma bonding here—or is there?

I casually walk into the kitchen to get a cup of coffee. One day, I spot a package on the table. "Surely it's my daughter's," I think. I look—it's for me. The return address is the rehab I was recently released from. Perplexed, I grab a knife to open the package up. It's a package of pills. I am now openly hostile at this situation. I went there to detox from pills, and now they are sending them to me. I think about our nation's preoccupation with prescriptions. My thoughts are racing. My heart is beating faster. I'm feeling sweaty. I am triggered beyond belief. I might be drinking, but at least I'm taking pills. Although what is inside is not considered a controlled substance, it's a mood stabilizer that is commonly abused and used on the street. It effectively melts your brain, making you so slurry that you need subtitles to be understood.

My anger at the pharmaceutical industry is palpable. I went to the doctor for headaches years ago and came out with a life-altering prescription. I took them responsibly for years, but the slippery slope of addiction took hold. I recall that America's addiction problem is much older than most people think. Some 200 years ago, laudanum was America's first documented addiction. Laudanum was a sleeping agent, rumored to have been abused by Mary Todd Lincoln.

With the advent of morphine, soldiers returning from the Civil War led to a new generation of addicts. It would only spiral from there: cocaine was invented to get the soldiers off morphine; heroin to get the nation off cocaine; crystal meth to get you off heroin...

President Taft was the first president to address the nation's cocaine problem. Federal regulations were then created so that these substances could no longer be sold in a general store. Eventually, the FDA would be created. Patrick Kennedy was picked up for driving high on Ambien. Tiger Woods just this year. Addiction is not just a poor man's disease! It's insidious, affecting every walk of life, for as far back as we've been keeping track.

In a slope so slippery, there is a pill for everything. Every day, commercials come on TV about how to fix this or that with pills. Overweight? There's a pill for that. Can't sleep? Look at our menu of pills. You will find something that tastes good. There is no thought that, maybe, you should just stop consuming high-fructose corn syrup to lose weight. There is no thought that you can read a book to fall asleep. The medical industrial complex has a hold on this country. Pressed for time, everyone wants the easy way out of a health problem, just as I do.

Emotional Intelligence has flown out the window in this country. There is no concept of delayed gratification; we need results yesterday. You realize that the Rolling Stones' song about "Mother's Little Helper" was just a reflection of the pharmaceutical revolution.

Anxiety pills destroyed my life. I was overprescribed antibiotics some 15 years ago, and it destroyed the lining of my bladder. This led to the stinging feeling of a bladder infection. The pain resulted in daily drinking — two small beers erased the uncomfortable sensation. Other antibiotics have caused intestinal paralysis. When the alcohol alone didn't work, I added sleeping pills. Ambien blackouts led to late-night drinking in bars when I thought I was home asleep. Every pill, instead of making me better, is making me ill. There was no thought at treating whatever the underlying condition was. It was just a Band-Aid. And a Band-Aid won't work when what you're trying to alleviate is the size of a bullet hole.

Somehow, this thinking is simultaneously occurring in the chaos of my mind. The cornucopia of pills has scrambled my brain. I can't stop thinking about pills. The obsession has now kicked in. Just can't stop the obsession. I count 17 prescriptions, at 30 pills each. I need sleep. I want my brain to be melted. I want the subtitles. I try redirecting myself. No, this isn't working... I am panicked... I am triggered... I am freaking the fuck out! I told myself that I was done with pills. I didn't need to be fully sober, just stay away from pills, and stick to beer; beer alone can't destroy my life, can it?

I decide to bag them up and throw them away. I know; I soon realized that putting them into the garbage can was not an option — too easy to simply retrieve them. I drive them to a dumpster around the corner and come home...and try to decorate my Christmas tree. But all I can think about is dumpster diving; apparently, a new hobby is being considered... I need some damn pills! I need a time dilation, where suddenly the obsession has passed. The pills are screaming at me from the dumpster. How could my day be hijacked by the mail?

I run upstairs to lay down with my boyfriend. Human contact is the only strategy I can think of. I urgently want him to fully wake up and just hold me. I want to tell my story urgently and compulsively. I started measured breathing... I hold on tight to Frank... I start evaluating the situation, just trying to calm down and not cave in. But time seems to have come to a halt. Before the mail came, pills hadn't crossed my mind for a while; now it's an all-consuming problem.

Little by little, things get better. I realize I need to run to the store. I will be driving past the dumpster. The pills are still screaming too loud! But I lay next to Frank a little longer, lay in here just a little longer. These are actual psychiatric medications to keep me functioning and operational, but I don't take them responsibly anyhow, so I shouldn't take them at all. Time passes a little more swiftly now. Laying down with Frank in a dark room really has calmed me down. I was getting dramatic for nothing! I knew it!

I think about how, now, the pills are useless to me. I remember how I joked with Frank that I would be discovering time travel before he got out of bed. It was two in the afternoon; what was he doing in bed anyway? Somehow, my mind went from being obsessed and helpless about the prescriptions to harassing Frank about napping, even though I had just been laying down with him moments before.

Journal Entry 2—The Suicide Solution

Hollywood has been shaken by recent suicides. Robin Williams, Chester Bennington, Chris Cornell, and Kate Spade seemed so happy even the day before they died. How could this happen? I am here to show you.

A timeline of a mental breakdown:

New Year's Eve I suffered a dissociative break from reality. I called 911 on myself three times in three days. The third time I was Baker Acted—pink-slipped, forced to stay in the hospital where the doors only go one way.

From New Year's Day to January 5th, I was in a psychiatric facility. I had my first real manic episode with psychotic features—but I was so manic that it took 7 sleep meds to get 90 minutes of sleep a night. Seven—it should've been enough to stop a heart or at least take down a horse. This is why you don't stop psychiatric medications without supervision. My brain was springing in all directions like a rubber band.

January 5th. I was discharged against the wishes of the doctor because I am lucky enough to afford a home health aide. (She was just a neighbor who needed money.) I really should've stayed longer. Besides the bipolar, I have severe PTSD from David. They needed more time for a full evaluation.

January 20th. I have an appointment with my long-time therapist, and she scales back my meds. Little did I know, she scaled them back too far, and the mania started rising again.

January 26th. I call the numbers I was given for humanistic counseling. The list was terribly out-of-date. Three people I called had retired; two more weren't accepting new patients. I found one in Hudson and left a message. I get a call back, and the woman is too confused to make an appointment—why, I don't know; I just needed an appt, and she works at a medical office. Ugh, no one knows how to do their job anymore.

January 29. Still trying to get an appt with a therapist. After they don't return my call, I tell them this is why there is a suicide solution and mass-shooting problem in this country. Obviously, I won't get a call back now.

January 30th. Call my longtime therapist, and her phone lines are down.

January 31st. I have two appointments scheduled— one with an addictions counselor and one with my family practitioner. They are at the same time. Stressed and confused from the lack of meds, I miss both, compounding the issue I'm trying to resolve.

February 2nd. I am losing it. I get meds from a friend. I call my family physician, and he doesn't call back.

February 3rd. I miss my therapist's appointment because, in a fit of rage, I tell her I am going to sue her. I get enough meds for a few days until I get in with a doctor. The next five days will be spent running back and forth, getting black-market meds. If no one will cooperate, I must take matters into my own hands.

February 5th. Go to Metro Health — I am told he would rather see me die than give me something like a mildly controlled substance. (In my panic, I forgot that the weed calmed me down.)

February 7th. I finally see a doctor; he gives me what I had been taking on the black market — it had been recommended. It works so perfectly with my other meds that this is the most normal I've ever felt in my life, and I owe it to my new best friend. He has no names of therapists either. The fact that these excessively strong medications make me feel normal is a red flag of addiction that was lost on me, but not the doctor in question.

By February 9th. I realize that I still need more meds, but my home-healthcare aide is back after I fired her. It's only been two days since I've seen the doctor, and I already need new medications.

February 10th. I get the wrong meds. (If I didn't know pharmacology, they would have killed me in one night!)

Look at how long I have persisted! But now, I will be running out of psych meds because my meds need to be adjusted. This could lead to a dissociative break. But it won't, I tell myself. During these breaks from reality, hallucinations occur. I hallucinated that my daughter was hunting me down once. If I had been a little less grounded, I could've really hurt someone because, in my mind, it was self-defense. I knew I had to do something, so I called 911 and locked myself up. Psych wards are much better these days, and it feels like summer camp.

February 10th. My home-health aide finds a therapist that is not accepting new clients. I'm still looking for a therapist. I call my family physician, and he doesn't call back. Any medical professional could take one look at me and know my requests were not truthful.

I forgot I bought counterfeit pressed pills! They should be here any day now. But the question, now, is: do they have fentanyl in them? I don't need a super Xanax! The slippery slope of one addictive pill has now led me to this.

Rock Bottom Number 3

So going off my pills was a bad idea.

The winter of 2018 was a rough one. After I went off my pills, I ended up in the psych ward twice, I was probated, and I was assigned a guardian ad litem. I had to report to court when I was probated, and they would ask me if I was taking my pills, feeding myself, and staying out of trouble. The whole episode was so scary I will never go off my pills again like that.

Realizing on New Year's Eve I went into the hospital after calling 911 on myself three times in three days. The first time, Savannah stopped them from taking me. The second time, I almost got shot by a police officer, and Frank jumped. I should mention I was hallucinating at this point. It was a very cold winter, and while running up the driveway, I thought my daughter Savannah was hunting me down. Once again, grateful there were no guns nearby. The third time, it was New Year's Eve, and I went to the casino. Frank was home sick from all the partying. I wanted to party like it was 1999. And then, I knew something was wrong. I ran out of the casino and told a police officer to call 911. They always ask, "Are you suicidal or homicidal?" I always want to say, "Not yet. Can't this be a preemptive strike?"

I was sent to a psych ward in Chardon. Once again, I knew someone there. A woman I met in rehab. I was running into all the same people in all the wrong places. At the ER, Holly and Bob come to visit. I was telling people I was going to be richer than Zuckerberg.

This psych ward was so much fun I called it summer camp. We even had lessons on songwriting. I shouldn't have left the hospital when I did, but no changing that now. I went back to a psych ward a month later. While at probate court, the judge asked one guy why the government wasn't allowed into his apartment, and he flat out said, "Because you'll find the hookers and drugs."

I had to go to a community health center—the people were so, so poor they didn't have shoes on their feet, only plastic bags from Dollar General.

When I went off the pills, I had a manic episode with psychotic features—so fancy. At times I felt like a demigod, and the whole time felt indestructible, but also caused destruction.

Getting guardian ad litem. I've now been probated. Spending money, having fun, and drinking like no tomorrow. But the meds have been kicking in for a month now. My brain is getting back to "normal." I begin to look through the wreckage of the bank account.

Ugh, this has been coming for a while now. There is no money; I mean absolutely no money—my retirement money is gone, Larry's retirement is gone, no money in the bank, credit card debt out the wazoo.

It had been weighing on my mind now that I'm getting sober. Getting to a 12-step meeting had been on my mind for a couple of weeks now.

I called Rose; it's May 5, 2018. Rose came over and cleared out all of the alcohol and took it my older daughter's house—I think she still has some of it. Then Rose took me to a 12-step meeting. I was nervous about Frank's reaction. He was golfing, and he had no idea that I woke and decided to get sober. I knew, if I drank that day, I would be drunk by the time he came home. He was such an enabler. Staying with him will kill me, in a misguided attempt to not disrupt his own drinking.

I would end up being sober about sixty days. I was on a pink cloud. I met a lot of people in AA, but it was very cliquish and like high school. I relapsed when I got my legal bill, which was almost fifty thousand dollars.

But that May 5, when I was all out of money and begging for food from food banks, I knew something had to change. Larry did not agree. About six weeks later, he would be in the ER because of his drinking.

I was on such a pink cloud when I quit drinking that time. I would describe that rest of the year as sober-ish.

Journal Entry from Summer of 2018

Why I can't drink—the preoccupation is ridiculous. I can't focus on getting things done because I'm wondering when I can have a drink. I have all these great jobs lined up, but they will only work if I'm sober. Eventually, there would be sick days. Remember, my work ethic sucks as it is. I need to give my job my all, within reason. Eventually I'd be too preoccupied by drinking to focus on my job. Then stuff wouldn't get done when I am at home because I'll be too tired from work. I'll need to make dinners. I don't want my appearance to suffer. I don't want it to be corporate serfdom all over again. Work, drink, asleep before 8—which is already happening.

This environmental education position is amazing. This could put me back on top. But, right now, I don't want to wait until after driver's ed to drink. Really, I just use it to pass the time. When time seems slow, I drink to pass the time, the way you pass the time with smoking. This preoccupation... I'm making more coffee.

Bourbon on Your Pancakes

Definition:
Idiom for day drinking.

Exemplification of Usage:
"Time flies when you pour bourbon on your pancakes."

It's 5:00 a.m., and I can't bear the thought of waiting until dinner to drink. That is over twelve hours away. The time is crawling as I watch the clock, waiting for it to be an acceptable hour to drink. Drinking at dinnertime is acceptable; having bourbon on your pancakes is not. There is no denying that I have a problem. For years, I lied to myself and told anyone who would listen that my drinking habits were normal. I would say, "People in Europe drink every day, and no one bats an eye." The fact that I wasn't living in Europe was beside the point. I was living in some sort of dystopian reality in which I was an addict and, oddly, the last to know.

I decided to pour some liquor in my coffee—just for flavor, of course. No one would know if I put a lil somethin' somethin' in my coffee. Five in the evening is just entirely too far away. All I can think about is relaxing with a drink, and the sun hasn't risen yet; the birds are not yet chirping. *It's always darkest before the dawn,* I tell myself. *I'm going to stop drinking someday, just not today. My drinking isn't even that bad. Bloody Marys are acceptable in the morning, but whiskey isn't? Who makes up these rules anyhow?*

Frank won't even be awake for hours, that lazy piece of shit. Now *his* drinking is a problem. The fifth of whiskey a day—his eyes are glazed over when he talks, he shouts over the smallest of inconveniences, and he does nothing around the house. This boy is a solid two, not even two and a half with respect to beauty. He was so funny when we first met, but the laughs have dried up, and this horrifying reality is setting in.

As soon as the whiskey in the coffee hits, I'll be able to think more clearly. *I do my best thinking with a little buzz,* I tell myself. *It's enhancing my life, really. I don't know why my family can't see that.*

Six a.m. is rolling around, and it's almost time to take my pills. The whiskey isn't working today—I'm sure some of Mommy's little helpers will do the trick. The pill bottle is close to empty; I need to contact some of my plugs. The fact that I have more than one plug is quite telling, but I'm the last to know everything. Why wouldn't I be the last to know I might die living this way?

By 7:00 a.m., I'm bordering on drunk. I'm trying to shower, but I'm wobbly. *This is perfect,* I think. *I can lay back down and get more sleep. Who wants to be awake for the day at 5:00 a.m. anyway?* See, I wasn't drinking in the morning; it's actually the middle of the night for me.

Suddenly, I feel a tightness in my throat, my chest, my mind. *Fuck! Not this again* — I'm not even sure what is happening, but when it happens, I'm an unbearable chaotic, quivering mess. I'm not lucid enough to know what is happening. The pills will help with this. They loosen me up. I just have too stressful a life to live it sober. I'm not even hurting anyone but me. If you were going through what I'm going through, you'd live like this too. I'm divorcing the biggest prick on the planet, I have no job, my kids won't talk to me, and I'm an orphan. Why wouldn't I need something to unwind?

Still, I can't help but think that the time to get sober is arriving. I've got a belly full of booze and a head full of people screaming at me about my "European" drinking habits. I'm told I'm too taxing to be friends with anymore. In fact, Frank is about the only one on the planet that will even speak to me lately, and I can barely tolerate his existence. This drinking is both expensive and an utterly forgettable experience. I wish I could pinpoint where my life went wrong. Could I have swerved in another direction to avoid being a dumpster fire of a hot mess? Was this collapse unavoidable?

I stare at the clock—it's approaching 8:00 a.m. Is it too early to switch to beer? I'll be on to shots by noon. Even with whiskey glasses on, I can tell that I have a problem. Isn't it unrealistic to go the whole, entire rest of my life without a drink? I mean, really? I don't think it's possible, I really don't. I'm not even that bad. It's not as if I'm a felon or something. It's not as if I'm homeless. It could be so much worse. It's just not a good time to quit drinking. I've got too much going on. When things settle down, I'll quit. Pretty soon, I'll get my life together. Just not today. It's almost time to pass out anyway. It's not even 10:00 a.m., and my overactive elbow has rendered me useless to leave the house.

What macabre existence is this? I'm a walking contradiction. I drink to relax but get more anxious. I drink to cure insomnia but awaken tired and restless. I drink to spur my creativity but pass out in my pancakes. I drink to wind down but end up on the other side of town for more festivities. I drink to be social, but I've never been more alone in my life. I drink...I drink...I drink.

I can hear Frank beginning to stir upstairs. I've got to get rid of this giant ball of Peter Pan syndrome with which I live. I can't even take care of myself, and I'm supposed to be taking care of him? He doesn't help with bills; he doesn't clean the house; he doesn't even know how to operate hand tools. He's as useless as tits on a bull. What did I see in this guy anyway? Before his whiskey sets in, he's supportive, kind, funny, and smart. Problem is, his whiskey is always there. Problem is, *my* whiskey is always there. We are enabling each other into early graves. We are toxic as hell for each other.

This buzz isn't pleasant at all. In fact, it's so unpleasant that I'm really thinking of turning my life around. I think I will quit drinking. Before I was a drunk, I earned a master's degree, and my kids loved me. I had friends and hobbies. I had a life before I became a barfly. I should quit drinking just to turn off the war inside my head. I'm my own best friend and my own worst enemy at the same time. I have no identity outside of the bottle to which I'm desperately clinging, and my world has become smaller than this bottle of booze. Oof, I think the time is near.

I'm feeling sick. I'm sick and tired of being sick and tired. I don't know how to live, and despite my best efforts, I don't know how to die. Bed spins are kicking in, and it isn't even time for *Let's Make a Deal* to begin. My day is shot before it begins. April showers have ended, and the sun is warm today; the new grass in the yard is an electrifying shade of green. But I'm too drunk to leave the house.

Frank is going to be pissed when he comes down the stairs, but, yeah, Frank is the problem. *Keep telling yourself that—you can't utter even a single sentence without contradicting yourself.* My stomach is turning and queasy; I'm heading to the bathroom—I think the whiskey is coming back.

Lights out for the day, and it's not yet noon. I need to stop listening to the bartender in my head.

Irish Goodbye

Definition:
Leaving a party or other special event without saying goodbye.

Exemplification of Usage:
Me: There is too much drinking at this party. I got to go.

Her: Say nothing to anybody; they won't remember anyhow. Just do an Irish goodbye.

On the March 18, 2020, my phone rang unexpectedly, but somehow, I knew what the call was about. The day was rainy, gloomy, and I was tired, though it was not yet quitting time on a Friday.

"Sue?" my brother Bob said quietly. "Dad was found dead in his condo today. We don't know what happened yet, but I hope he went quickly."

I knew this was coming, but still had always hoped I would have more time. I immediately felt pangs of regret for not making more time for my father, and I replayed our last conversation in my head. When I saw him two weeks before, he had given me a hug that I'll never forget. That hug should have tipped me off. I had only ever received two hugs from him before. Did he orchestrate this eternal Irish goodbye, or did he die peacefully? His drinking had been so problematic of late that I was unsure.

Reflections on growing up with my father, who was an astronomer, filled my mind. Conversations about constellations, quasars, and the Big Bounce start creeping into my mind. His colorful trips to Tibet, Moscow, and Cuba leave me wishing I had asked more questions, or at the very least, recorded what was said. His tales of drinking in Harlem, studying at Columbia University, and building his own scuba equipment after reading an article in *Popular Mechanics* leave me in awe at his amazing yet troubled life. His home in Amherst, his hoarding, and his generally unkempt demeanor of late tortured me. He was too smart for his own good. I was grateful that he was no longer torturing himself over unfixable problems, past regrets, and plans for the future that disappeared with his last breath.

My feelings are just as confusing now as when he was alive. Was he an inspiration to his students or a destructive Communist? At times, he seemed to have many identities. Was there a single William Dent? All hope of future conversations vanished in one phone call. But, like me, sometimes he was an intelligent hero; other times, the perpetual victim with a sob story for everything. I hadn't seen the bully side of him in some time.

The urgency of the situation and the things that needed to be accomplished were overwhelming—notifying my boss, preparing substitute lesson plans, contacting my daughters, and contacting a funeral home. Not two feet from me, a student sat waiting for direction from me while I tried to process the phone call. My father wanted to be cremated, but he had purchased a plot at Crown Hill Cemetery—his directions for his last wishes were as conflicted as he.

Breathe in; breathe out. These things take time. I felt shocked and betrayed.

I needed to get home to Frank. Would he be a shoulder to cry on, or would today be yet another day that he had an axe to grind with the world? Would he be supportive, or would he get blackout drunk? Our relationship had been deteriorating as I'd begun to realize he couldn't possibly take care of me when he couldn't even take care of himself. His daily pints of Jameson were taking a toll on us. His anger was unpredictable. His personal problems were mounting. What started off as fun and games was quickly leading me to another rock bottom.

I found myself wishing my dad had lived to see me sober. Would I live to see myself sober? Time seemed to be running out. In three months, I had quit my job in a fit of anger, gone to rehab, relapsed, and now this. I didn't have money for groceries; how would I pay for a funeral? Did my father have money set aside for his funeral? I had one hundred questions and no one to ask. How was I going to stay sober under these circumstances? My father was the last person in my corner, my biggest fan, but now he was gone. He was my biggest fan and he's gone. He was so many things...and now he's gone.

Too emotional to drive or mingle at the bar, I headed home and frantically began looking for my pills. Was there beer in the house? What would become of me now that I was an orphan? Frank and I needed to break up. I needed to get sober. I needed to sort my life out once and for all. My last supporter was dead.

I knew what Frank was going to say. This wasn't the time to worry about cutting costs. This wasn't the time to reinvent myself. This wasn't the time for anything but bar-hopping and reminiscing. This wasn't the time to worry about the future. He was going to take care of me in the future—he just needed to sort his life out.

I'd been questioning for months how either of us would sort out our lives over fifths of whiskey. Our heads were never clear enough to make any forward momentum in our lives. All we seemed to be doing was moving backwards.

I opened the back door to see all the dirty dishes that had piled up throughout the week. My house was a mess; my life was a mess; my mind was a mess. I could feel a fight coming on with Frank, and he didn't even know half of what I was going through. He hadn't received even a text from me yet.

I told myself to grab a beer and two pills, and things would get better. Hadn't I been saying this to myself for a decade now? That solution hadn't been working for some time. In fact, it was taking me in the opposite direction from where I wanted to go.

Frank startled me as he walked in early from work.

"Sorry, baby, work was slow, so they sent me home."

"Frank, we need to talk. My dad died today. We have no money; we must quit drinking. There is no money for beer. We are in danger of losing the house."

"Baby, there is always money for beer."

"Don't 'baby' me. We're broke. It's time to grow up. I'm forty-eight—this is long overdue."

"Baby, your dad passed today; this isn't the time."

"When is the time, Frank? When *exactly* is the time? At the food bank? When we lose the house? When the IRS comes knocking at our back door?"

"Shit, baby, I should've just stayed at work if this is how you're going to be."

"Move out, Frank! Move the fuck out! You're the kind of help that nobody needs."

"Where is all of this coming from? I thought things were going so well."

"Well, you thought wrong."

"Thanks, Susan, thanks. Thanks for ruining my weekend before it even started. I've been looking forward to putting my feet up all week and now this."

"All you've done your whole life is put your feet up. Grow the fuck up, and get out of my house!"

"Susan, you're just upset. You really are a head case, aren't you?"

"My died dad today. You are a thorn in my side who's of no help to anyone, including yourself. For the last time, get the fuck out and stay out!"

"Don't you want me to help to plan the services?"

"How can you plan the services, Frank? You don't even know how to work a checking account? For the last time, get the fuck out, or I call the cops."

"Fine, Susan, fine. I've been nothing but good to you. Does this mean the wedding is off?"

Not even shocked by the stupidity, I push Frank out the door and sit down with my beer, turn on the TV, and promise myself, once again, to sort my life out tomorrow. I begin to cry. I will never see my father alive again; he was my last supporter.

Desert Camping

Definition:
What you tell your boss you were doing when you were really serving a three-day jail sentence because of a DUI.

Exemplification of Usage:
Me: Boss, I can't come in this Saturday.

Him: Why not?

Me: I had a desert-camping weekend scheduled before I took this job.

If there was any question in my mind that I had a "real" problem, that doubt should've disappeared when I arrived at a halfway house on the outskirts of Cleveland. My "at leasting" was out of control during my time at that halfway house. "At leasting" is when you compare yourself out of recovery—he has five drunk-driving charges; at least I'm not that bad. She lost her kids; at least I'm not that bad.

She drank while she was pregnant; at least I'm not that bad. I drink alcohol, and that's legal; at least it's not heroin. As you can see, this can go on for hours.

Instead, think of these as "yets." I haven't been arrested... yet. I haven't lost my kids...yet. I haven't done heroin...yet. As I sat in that halfway house, convincing myself I didn't have a problem, there were so many yets that hadn't happened. I did get arrested. I did do meth. I did lie, cheat, and steal from family for money. I did do terrible things to supply myself with drugs and alcohol. I lost friends; I damn near lost my life.

But at the halfway house, I kept finding all the differences, pointing out flaws with twelve-step programs and halfway-house living in general. As a general rule, psychiatric medications were prohibited in halfway houses. Those people were not doctors and should not have withheld medicine from twenty-five newly sober girls, but they did. I knew that, without my psych meds, I stood no chance at all of being sober long-term. The halfway house relied on food donations for us to eat; if no one donated food, we didn't eat. It was an untenable situation. The house didn't even have locking doors. One of the residents had to stay up all night, protecting the house from intruders—we were in inner city Cleveland. We had no weapons and no access to a telephone. If a one-armed, axe-wielding maniac had shown up, we had no way to defend ourselves or call for help. It was dysfunctional as hell, and

I was supposed to get better there? Unmedicated, unsafe, and an unreliable food supply? Not likely.

There were women who confessed to exchanging sexual favors for money; I told myself, *At least I'm not that bad.* However, addiction is progressive, chronic, and can be fatal. If I kept using, I *could* be that bad. Your addiction progresses a lot like child-rearing—it gets progressively harder. When your baby is born, you're changing diapers and bottle feeding, and you think, *This is the hard part; surely it gets easier.* Then your child is a toddler, and you're trying to keep the child from accidentally dying by preventing them from running with scissors or playing in the road, and you think, *This must be the hard part.* Then the teenage years come along, and a person with a squeaky voice, pimples, and body odor thinks you're embarrassing to be seen with, and you think, *It doesn't get easier until they leave.*

Addiction is the same way. In the early stages, you think, *This isn't so bad; I just need to get back on track.* Then, as it progresses, you think, *Okay, this is the hard part, but some mental calculations will crack the code, and I'll be back on track. I'll solve this puzzle and go back to the good times.* Then, finally, you're embarrassed to be seen with your drug of choice and realize the only hope for normalcy is when it leaves your life. The few alcoholics I have seen throttle back their addiction just transferred it to shopping and gambling. These people will look you in the eye and tell you that they just woke up one day and were no longer dealing with a substance-abuse problem. Meanwhile, the gambling and shopping is driving them into bankruptcy, making them lose friends, and causing their families to disown them. Addiction comes in many forms. It does not have to be injected into your body.

While the twelve-step detox, long-term rehab, and halfway house didn't work for me the way they wanted it to, I learned many valuable lessons. My favorite advice from twelve-step programs is to refrain from making any big decisions for a year. This has kept me out of a relationship, and that has been a blessing, as I have more issues than I realized. The program got me started on my codependency issues, for instance, and that's invaluable. When you have an addiction problem, it's not as if your brain is fully functional and just the addiction part of the brain is misfiring. No, when you're addicted, your whole brain is misfiring. Your work ethic stinks, you're inattentive, unloving, selfish, and dishonest. No part of your brain is fully optimal.

One memory that sticks out surely should have made me realize I had a very serious problem; it occurred in the med line at rehab. During a medicated detox, which I highly recommend, you may be given Valium to stop the shakes, lower your blood pressure, and help you sleep. I didn't feel I was getting enough Valium; I didn't even think I had a problem, so why wouldn't I want more Valium? In the med line, how sweaty you were determined how likely it was that you needed Valium. I made sure I seemed sweaty.

I licked my palms so my hands were sweaty, put my fore-head under the lamp so that it was hot, and sprinkled water on my temples for additional sweat. The fact that I did all this just to get one pill shows how deep my problems really were. Then I bragged about pulling one over on the psych med nurse—ahh, good times. Selfish, deceitful, and con-trolling behavior, in addition to the compulsion for a pill.

As I bounced in and out of recovery for two years, I kept seeing the same faces at all the wrong places. Upon arrival at the psych ward, I recognized people from rehab. Upon arrival at drug court for a urine sample, I again saw ladies from rehab. I saw the same people at twelve-step meetings that I saw in a bar the next day. We were all on the same relapse-and-disease progression circuit. Unfortunately, many of the people whom I met in these places are no longer alive, victims of their addiction because they believed that there was no way out, that abstinence wasn't in the cards for them. I personally think they just didn't have the right tools.

My program is holistic—sobriety coaching, psych meds, therapy, physical exercise, and proper nutrition. Each piece is very important. I found focusing on my gut health helped to eliminate my panic attacks. Cheap dyes in cheap food were contributing to my anxiety. The physical exer-cise helps to moderate my invisible disabilities. My health feels like a full-time job at times, but I've already seen the effects of ignoring my needs and am not willing to go back to that—ever.

Being admitted multiple times to psych wards, detox units, and rehabs; getting arrested; my liver swelling; seizures from excessive use; facing homelessness—these all became the yets of addiction that turned into a realities. Several overdoses, licking my palms for pills, stealing from family—it's ridiculous to think that I thought I didn't have a problem. Please, do not read this and think, *At least I'm not that bad; see, I don't need to quit.* That would mean you're missing the whole point of this chapter. Quit while you're ahead. It will never return to recreational use. Even if you tell yourself that you're hurting no one but yourself, then I must ask, why are you so intent on hurting yourself? Sobriety won't be easy in the beginning, but I promise you that it's worth it.

I'm now teaching at a college, volunteering with teenagers in foster care, and have a side business quilting. I live in a beautiful home, have the best finances of my life, and my friendships aren't one-sided. There's a distinct lack of drama, of chaos, and when you're not used to it, a peaceful life can seem boring. The reality is that you're so used to chaos, fight-or-flight, fawn, and freeze that you know no other way of living. Life really begins when you realize you only get one shot at this life. If the way your life is going now were to stay that way until you pass, would you be all right with that? And realize that life, like parenting and addiction, gets progressively harder. Jobs come with more responsibilities. You may have to take care of your parents in their old age. My life certainly kept getting more difficult, and it was only in sobriety that I was up for the challenge.

Two Licks
and a Promise

Definition:
When a girl is drunk, and she says she's going to give you a blow job, but all you get is two licks and a promise.

Exemplification of Usage:
Him: I was sexually frustrated in that relationship. She didn't like giving head, and she was drunk all the time, so all I got was two licks and a promise.

It was a random, ordinary day with Killian, but there is an unexpected joy in living an ordinary life. You just have to have the attitude that the grass is greener where you water it, and not on the other side of the fence. Killian is the guy who made me realize why things never worked out with anyone else. When Johnny Cash was asked what heaven was like, he said, "With her, having coffee." That's how I felt about Killian.

One lesson I learned along the way is that it is not enough to love someone; you need to love yourself as well when you're with them. But I digress. It was simple day of getting a bite to eat, riding on his motorcycle, and people watching during karaoke. It was what I call a sparkle day. Not many sparkle days come around, what with work, cleaning, and bills, so when a sparkle day shows up, I don't soon forget it.

The day started with Killian expressing to me that he wanted to spend the day with me and take me on his bike. He has a white Harley-Davidson that is full of chrome and hand-printed pinstriping. It's a real showstopper. He loves his bike; he likes to wander, as I do. I can't quite explain it, but when you wander, your problems at home seem to work themselves out both metaphorically and physically. He calls decompressing on his bike wind therapy. Now that I've gotten a taste of wind therapy, I like it.

It was an unseasonably warm Wednesday in March, and neither of us wanted to waste the beautiful Ohio day. I put on my black lace-up boots to keep my feet safe and my flowered leather jacket to keep me both warm and safe. Just because you're having fun, doesn't mean you shouldn't be responsible.

We also wanted to get a bite to eat, as well as get some wind therapy in, so we drove through the metro parks to take advantage of the scenic routes offered. The windy, forested roads are both fun to drive and beautifully scenic. We headed south, away from the city, in search of food. We were forest bathing on a Harley. As we approached our intended destination, we saw that it was closed for repairs.

We ended up at a place called the County Line Saloon. We chatted, ate our food, which was delicious, and headed to our next stop, which was the Tavern on Broadway. Our main activity at TOB was supposed to be karaoke, but it ended up being a lesson on people watching for me. It was a lot of fun.

The DJ doing the karaoke ended up with a situation that was not unlike every sitcom you've ever seen. He was dating two girls at the same time, and they both showed up that night to see him. Just watching him trying to process what to do was hilarious. I don't try to laugh at another's pain, but if you're dumb enough to date two girls from the same town at the same time, you get what you deserve.

There were so many people looking to hook up that night at karaoke that it became kind of a people-watching game to see who was going to hook up with whom. Who was getting shot down, and who was going home alone. I've never been much of a people watcher, but Killian is.

As a former bouncer, his job was to watch people and anticipate their next move; he knows people but has fun with it. I laughed so much at this newfound game of people watching before the night's end.

With Killian, I finally felt as if I had met someone on my same intellectual level. We stayed up sometimes until 4:00 a.m., lying around naked, talking, watching TV, and other activities. On the weekends, we had the best date nights that I had ever had with anyone. Since I was sober, I remembered them all too. We went to art exhibits, we went downtown to eat, and we went to concerts in the park. It was, hands down, the best summer of my life. I hadn't had that much fun since my courtship with David.

And that's when I started noticing some of the red flags. There seemed to be a lot of mixed messages about where our relationship was going. He continuously mentioned that all his exes were crazy. I never stopped to ask what he did to make his exes crazy. He mentioned that his dating luck wasn't good, as he always started dating a girl just two months before she self-destructed. I never considered that he was a contributing factor in their self-destruction.

At this time, I was fairly new at sobriety and didn't have much money. I'm just grateful that I didn't lose my home, my life, or my daughters during addiction. It's just nice to know that you don't have to be rich or famous to enjoy life. It's just nice to know that the best days of your life haven't happened yet. Sometimes, you just need to be reminded to find joy in the ordinary and that there are sparkle days ahead. Remember, the grass is greener where you water it, not on the other side of the fence. In this case, Killian was watering his grass everywhere. I would find out soon enough that he was still a player, but with Waffle House money. By seven months into dating, he had lost his job, but that was the least of it. I felt as if I was getting abused in the same way I did with David—there was abuse present, but I couldn't pinpoint it.

Psychological abuse is like a gas leak; by the time you are one hundred percent sure there is a problem, the damage has been done. Unfaithful, abusive, and unemployed—no bigger deal-breakers if you tried. I felt as though I was catfished. The person at the end was not even remotely the person I met seven months ago. Everything he had ever said was nothing more than two licks and a promise.

Black Thumb

Definition:
The male equivalent of a black widow. A toxic, narcissistic man who is poisonous to everyone he encounters, much like Henry VIII. His heart is as black as the underworld, and he's as attractive as a thumb—hence, a black thumb.

Exemplification of Usage:
Her: Are you still dating Killian?

Me: That guy is a black thumb. I'm embarrassed I ever dated him.

Falling in love with a musician is particularly dumb, even for me. Truth be told, I was just looking for a booty call, as I had just gotten out of two relationships with men who were not fulfilling any physical needs. I wouldn't realize until later that I'm a relationship addict, and transfer addiction was setting in. I was early in sobriety and not comfortable in my own skin. Honestly, I didn't even realize that he was a musician or a felon. I didn't realize it because he withheld that information.

We became friends, dated, and eventually fell in love for a minute. I'm not the first girl to fool around and fall in love, and I won't be the last. At the end of the day, we had different values, morals, and expectations from a real relationship. He considered me the flavor of the week, as if I were ice cream you pick up from the store.

My self-esteem was in the toilet when I approached him in 2020 to be my boyfriend. When he rejected my offer, I told my friend he must've said no because he thought I was a cheap slut. My friend replied, "You think Killian thinks YOU'RE a cheap slut? He's fucked his way across the country!" Sad, but true. I thought I could turn a musician into a boyfriend for about one minute, but too many holes in his stories and problems came up instantly after we said, "I love you."

The bullshit meter had been off the charts of late, and I decided to ask Killian where he thought this relationship was going.

He responded with, "Too much, too soon."

I agreed and said, "There are way too many problems this early into getting to know someone."

He was shocked. "Are you breaking up with me? Why are you overreacting like this?"

"Am I overreacting, Killian, or is this a normal reaction to being strung along, receiving mixed messages, all of your exes being crazy, your disinterest in meeting my needs, being breadcrumbed, disrespected, and lied to? We are not even remotely compatible in the outside world, Killian, not even close."

"You know, your guard is up higher than you realize, Sue; you never even let me in. I feel like I barely know you."

"The sad part is that I've grown up in front of your eyes, and you didn't even realize it. Why would I let you in when you are one giant red flag?"

"I'm one giant red flag? What about you, Sue? What about your red flags?"

"What about mine, Killian? What about mine? I've been working on mine. I quit drinking, quit pills, cut up my credit cards. I hike in the park, go to therapy. We don't do any of the same things. You've been sitting at the bar for months, complaining about being at rock bottom."

"It sounds like you're breaking up with me."

"I am, Killian. I am. You haven't given me the respect a dog gives a tree. We've been seeing each other for seven months. I can't even get a happy-birthday or a ten-dollar Christmas present."

"See, you are too materialistic for me!"

"Grow up—it's the thought that counts! If you don't celebrate holidays, that just means we have different values."

"You're breaking up with me on New Year's Eve! You're ruining my holidays because I ruin yours! How petty is that, Sue? How petty is that!"

"When a man wastes seven months of my time, I'm going to be petty!"

"Oh, so now I'm a waste of time!"

"Pretty much!"

"Sorry I couldn't be the man you wanted me to be, Sue. I really am."

"Never underestimate…never. Not after the hell I've been through."

"See, we do have a lot in common. I went to the school of hard knocks too!"

"This isn't a pissing contest, Killian. I need a sober guy with a job, Killian, a job. You've been laying on the couch for months. I was fine before I met you, and I'll be fine long after you're gone!"

"Can't we talk about this, Sue?"

"No, we are incompatible! I live like a monk, and you live like a street urchin! Go back to the sewer rats you're used to. I'm no sewer rat, and it's sad you ever thought I was."

"I'm sorry, Sue. I'm sorry. Can we try again in six months after I get my shit together?"

"No, Killian, we can't. Goodbye for good this time. By the looks of it, it'll take a lot longer than six months for you to get your shit together."

"Where is all of this coming from, Sue?"

"Listening to you talk. You always pick girls that aren't available for real relationships; you pick ones that value their sobriety or drinking, or they're married. You pick women who put you in second place and then complain about it! You thrive on being a victim, Killian—absolutely thrive on it! It's old and irritating!"

"I don't know why I do the things that I do—you are acting like I meant to hurt you!"

"That's because you knew...you knew it would end this way. You always knew it."

"Sue...I thought we would move to the country one day...do the white-picket-fence thing."

"Why would I do that with you, Killian? Why? You treat me like an irritating stray dog that followed you home!"

"How can you say that? I've been nothing but nice to you!"

"Listen, we have nothing in common—you don't even like me, let alone love me. What in the Stockholm syndrome is going on here? You don't want me, but you don't want anyone else to have me? I'm being loyal to you, but I never have any idea where you're at lately."

"I'm sorry, Sue. I really am!"

"Goodbye, Killian!"

This was by the far the worst breakup I had ever been through. Killian, unknowingly, had created a trauma bond between us. Breaking a trauma bond is one of the most debilitating experiences I have ever encountered. It's physically, emotionally, and mentally painful. The fact that I can survive the withdrawal from a broken trauma bond while sober impresses even me.

Aftershocks

Definition:
When the negative effects of an abusive relationship show up long after it is over.

Exemplification of Usage:
I hate how I can't trust anyone and look over my shoulder all the time. It's the damn aftershocks.

The aftershocks of abuse by a narcissist are debilitating. Narcissists promise a dream and deliver a nightmare. Killian was no exception. In fact, he was worse than David in some ways. He brought new levels of pain to my life. As Killian inflicted terror, it brought many buried issues to the surface, including memories with David I had suppressed. It was similar to smacking a sunburn; Killian knew just where to hit to allow my issues to take the lead, so our issues seemed less significant. This insult hits an unknown wound from eighth grade; that insult hits a wound from college. He was better at psychological warfare than David.

After all the stories I heard from Killian about growing up abused, I should've known that I would be the next one abused. He said more than once that we are all products of our circumstances.

"You look like you woke up in Auschwitz!" This was a comment from my now ex-husband. It was during a very stressful time in my life, and this comment certainly did not help my self-esteem. I've always been on the thin side—just genetically lucky, really—so when life gets stressful, and I'm too upset to eat, my weight plunges dangerously low. This can be just as hard on your heart as obesity. People are jealous of thin women, but I had body dysmorphia thanks to all the skinny shaming. This is the kind of abuse prevalent in narcissistic behavior—insults targeted at your specific insecurities and core values.

About a week later, "So when did you start dressing like a n@gg3r?" David said.

"Wait! What? WHAT DID YOU JUST SAY? No, don't repeat that word ever!"

"What is your problem? I just mean you wear two pairs of pants now, just them n—"

"Don't ever say that word again. You know that word is not allowed in this house!"

"You say hillbilly all the time. That's just as racist!"

Talk about emotional whiplash. *What the fuck is this guy's problem?* I'm shaking my head in disbelief for more reasons than I can even figure out. "On what planet is the word 'hillbilly' even as remotely bad. The word you used was the last word they heard before their house was burned down, the last word they heard before they were raped, the last word they heard before their babies were stolen—"

"Gawd, I don't even know what your problem is—you're making a scene for no reason!"

Well, if that wasn't calling the kettle black. With those two insults, he revealed so much more than he could ever realize. By admitting that I looked no healthier than a concentration-camp victim or no healthier than a plantation slave, that meant, to beat me down, he was behaving like a slave master and concentration-camp guard. When I was losing my teaching job, he told the principal he could talk me into killing myself so that he wouldn't have to pay spousal support, and the school wouldn't have to worry about severance pay. That's just how evil he truly was. I kept saying he was a monster, and at every turn, he was proving me right. He was proving it in a game I so desperately wanted to be wrong and lose. He was as disturbed as any cult leader or demagogue the world has ever known. I was staring into the face of evil, and he still thought he was a catch I should be proud of. That silent tiger waiting to pounce when you're down—if he had barked like a dog from the start, I would've been scared off. But no, he was a shark, and he smelled blood. Time to go in for the kill.

If I thought it was bad with David, it was downright awful with Killian. Killian's abuse was so subtle you'd almost miss it if you didn't know what you were looking for. Killian took specific insecurities and used them against you; without the backstory, a bystander wouldn't even be able to tell you were being abused. It's as though you confided that you feel insecure about not being white-collar, and the abuser points to white-collar girls and says, "Look at those white-collar hotties. Good thing you're not like that." Very subtle, under-the-radar abuse, and in the example I used, you're left wondering if it was intentional, or if you're overly sensitive, which is why this type of abuse is so damaging. Since it's under the radar, at first, you can't prove anything wrong has been done...until you've received about 1,000 under-the-radar messages to your psyche, the damage has been done, and you're more insecure than ever. I was surrounded by bullies in childhood; turned out adulthood was no different.

***

Returning to David's comment—I was manic, drinking more than I was eating, and getting no real nutrients when David was mocking my weight. Instead of trying to alleviate the stress by feeding me, he insulted me at an already-low point in my life. Compounding the problem was the fact that, starting at a very early age, I had been internalizing negative remarks. I could be told I was smart one hundred days in a row, but the one day I attracted an insult, well, that day would live in infamy. I had a potential boyfriend in high school tell me that my boobs were smaller than his mother's, and she had had a double mastectomy.

Compounding all this was that I had grown up during a time and in a place that it was embarrassing to be smart. I think Zuckerberg and Elon have changed all that, but, growing up, I was routinely ridiculed for being at the head of the class. That led to many undesirable aftershocks. What do I mean by aftershocks? It's when, after the abuse, someone is being nice, but you feel as if it's a setup, the beginning of another con, another ruse that will leave you sick to your stomach once again. It's when you receive a compliment but remember only the previous abuse. It's when you begin the self-doubt, the mistrust of your ability to judge the character of a person. Are we at the beginning of a relationship? Or is this when the lobster is being placed into lukewarm water, only to reach a rolling boil in a few short months? Are we at the beginning of a relationship that won't die from one spectacular event, but from one thousand smacks to a sunburn?

When your self-esteem can find shade in the shadow of a snow pea, it has a ripple effect across your life. You date down, for one, picking up stray cats instead of established men. You drink for liquid courage; you drink to improve your self-image. Why not? Doesn't everyone look cool sipping a martini? You spend all kinds of money you don't have on clothes to make yourself look better. But the problem with low self-esteem is that you can spend, drink, and screw like a rabbit, but at the end of the day, you will still have low self-esteem. In fact, those very activities can make your low self-esteem worse.

This is what happened during my addiction and abuse. I was continually told I was a piece of shit, so I became a piece of shit. It becomes a self-fulfilling prophecy, and then the abuser looks at you and says, "See, I told you—you are a piece of shit." Then you drink some more because, well, you are a piece of shit. You drink to silence the mental termites in your brain that tell you that you are a burden to anyone who tries to love you.

My second husband, David, became the bane of my existence. After a whirlwind courtship, we married only six months after we met. He asked for a divorce for the first time on our *fourth* day of marriage because I forgot to say please when asking him to pass the butter. I remember thinking that I should just go for the divorce right then, but I was too embarrassed to get divorced four days after the wedding.

It was abundantly clear that he wished he'd never met me. He liked the way I looked, he liked my money and ambition, but he never really liked me as a person. And he made it known with the unrelenting abuse, control, and mind games. His policy during fights was total escalation. We never had a fight that he didn't want to turn into World War III. There is no point fighting if the end game is complete annihilation. Trust me, the end of the relationship *was* complete annihilation.

At every turn, he destroyed attempts to improve the quality of our lives. Cancelling Christmas, fighting on vacations, ruining plans for the family at the condo. Advancing in my career, birthdays, and on and on. It makes you physically ill. It destroys your mental health. As you get sucked into their materialism, it destroys your finances. When all that is combined, your spirituality is dead in the water.

* * *

One time during a particularly stressful holiday season, he cancelled Christmas. He took all the ornaments off the tree and dragged the tree to the curb, telling the kids that there would be no Christmas because he didn't like the tone of my voice. The tone of my voice is what caused all this terror. The kids were screaming and crying, distraught beyond any point of being able to console them. He couldn't calm down either, so he decided to leave the country for a week. This was before cell phones, and he was missing in Canada somewhere. Plagued by money and food insecurities, I was in no condition to calm down the kids, as I myself was hanging by a thread. Lost on him was that it was Christmas Day, and we were supposed to be celebrating a family holiday with a family he clearly never wanted. It was the holidays, my husband was missing, my children had been terrorized, and my husband had taken all our money with him, so I don't know how I'm going to pay the bills. I don't even know how I'm going to buy groceries if he doesn't return. This entire incident occurred because of my tone of voice; I had spoken in a grumpy manner.

I wish I could say that he was just having a bad day, but our whole marriage was like that. I walked on eggshells and lived in fear. It was a guns-and-roses relationship. During the acute incidents, he pulled out a gun sometimes, not really threatening me, just threatening to kill himself because I had ruined his life, and he wanted me to watch him kill himself. It was sheer psychological warfare. Then after I said that he needed help and that I was leaving, the bouquet of roses showed up along with promises to improve and professions about my being an angel who only improved his life. I had married Dr. Jekyll and Mr. Hyde.

The biggest problem, however, in surviving that kind of abuse is the aftershocks, not the least of which is dating after you've been treated like that. That treatment changes the way you look at the world, it creates trust and commitment issues, and it leaves you feeling even more damaged than before the relationship began. The flashbacks of horror show up in the middle of a good day. Masking the flashbacks is impossible. The subconscious message is that you're unlovable and a burden, so why bother to look or ask for better treatment. Again, Killian was the worst of all, taking copious amounts of time to end the abuse even after the breakup. He harassed me on social media and showed up at my work. I had to get the police involved. He sent numerous flying monkeys. I became so rattled by the post-separation abuse that I didn't even stay at my own home.

After the divorce, I couldn't believe that men just simply enjoyed my company. I hadn't realized that I didn't have to be perfect, a workhorse, or always on. I was allowed to relax and enjoy myself sometimes. I was allowed to have friends, nights out, and, God forbid, me time. But the aftershocks threaten to ruin future relationships because abused people will often unintentionally become abusers. It's just the way it works.

The real kicker of that relationship with David is that I learned to drink to keep my mouth shut. Voicing my opinion only led to fights and calls to 911. So I drank to shut up; I drank to keep the peace. The more I drank, the more he hated me. When I asked for sex, he gave me ten reasons he wouldn't even screw me for practice; then he wondered why I eventually had an affair.

I wasn't being emotionally supported. I was being destroyed, and my self-esteem and drinking problem only got worse. And for some reason, when he finally left me, I was devastated. I wanted to grow old with this man. This is how insidious abuse is. You develop a sort of Stockholm syndrome in which you love your abuser. You are conditioned into silence, submission, and dysfunction, and are told you are nothing without them. I thought my life was over when he left me. I begged him to come back. I stalked him, even to the point that I was arrested. I had literally lost my marbles trying to get my abuser to love me. It's a trauma-bonded relationship with the underlying message being, "You broke me, and you're the only who can fix me." But with every attempt to fix me, he broke me even worse. As with breaking a horse's spirit, you're never the same. I can't believe I even got out alive.

You know you have been in a relationship with a narcissist when you are physically, emotionally, financially, and spiritually destroyed. And yet they go on as if they haven't missed a beat.

The worst part of it all though? If you don't get help, you'll find a warm, loving, caring man who only wants the best for you, and you will accidentally become his abuser. Those aftershocks are a bitch. You're infested with narcissistic fleas and act like your abuser sometimes. Then you become physically ill as you recognize you have those fleas.

Breakups with a narcissist are different in many ways. I experienced what was called the reverse discard with both men. You are treated like shit in hopes that you will leave. Then when you leave, they call you crazy and say it's the best relationship you've ever been in. Both stalked me after the breakup, guilt-tripped me to the point of intense internal pain. Both involved lawyers and police. To the narcissist, the failure of the relationship is one hundred percent your fault. Some days, they beg you to come back, but other days tell you that you are the worst thing that ever happened to them. They try to convince you that you've made a mistake. They still want your undivided attention, even after the breakup.

Then the smear campaign starts. They give new meaning to the word "irony" by wanting to appear independent but acting really needy. The final stab to the heart is when you find out that they were cheating on you the whole time. You've endured all this pain for a man who never valued you enough to be exclusive. Mental termites, physical abuse, infidelity, missing money, and then—poof!—they're gone, and you're replaced within days. An idyllic courtship turns into emotional whiplash. It's similar to being in a car crash; things change that quickly.

If I've learned one thing in dating since the divorce, it is that dating a high-value man has nothing to do with job titles or money. A high-value man has a great work ethic, looks on the bright side of everything, and knows the value of a dollar and how to treat a woman. Don't get caught up in job titles, greed, or anything else that can disappear overnight. A good man's character won't disappear overnight. If he is genuine, he is a *consistent* person, not a romance artist one day and a bully the next. His gentlemanly ways will be there even on the day of your worst fight. That's how you know you have a keeper. He'll take your bad days in stride if you apologize, and with the right man, your self-esteem will improve. When my relationships with Frank and my first husband ended, I was actually in a better place. I no longer had to beg for attention or sex or call 911 regularly. That's not love at all. It's psychological terrorism, and I had become a prisoner of war twice.

Once it's over, truly over, the detoxing from the relationship begins, as does the victim blaming. You begin to realize how much you let slide. The abuse escalates slowly, like that lobster in a pot of boiling water. Each individual day isn't so bad for the most part, but they collect and become a death by one thousand paper cuts. After having been in fight-or-flight mode for so long, with intermittent good days that required constant fawning, your body begins shutting down. After about three months of no contact, when you begin to feel safe again, it might seem as if you were in freeze mode for weeks at a time, unable to function most days. It's so insidious because it affects every part of your life—your mental and physical health, your career, your finances, your friendships, your family relationships. It's total devastation of your life for a man who was never faithful to you. It's quite honestly the most painful thing I've ever gone through in my life, and that's saying something because I watched my mother die in front of me. Meeting Killian and David was worse than even that.

These relationships leave you with a level of mistrust and disdain for people that you never had before. After a relationship like this ends, you can do one of two things—focus on the abuse, or focus on yourself so this never happens again. After David, I focused on the abuse. After

Killian, I focused on myself. I realized that David, Killian, and my father were all the same person. My father was emotionally neglectful toward me, not outright abusive. But there so many other similarities. As with these two, my father seemed like three different people—the bully, the victim, and the hero. During my long trip in California with my father, I was physically ill much of the time. I didn't miss the red flags; they just felt like home— warm and comfortable while simultaneously stabbing me in the back. With new levels of horror, I now realize what my mother endured during her relationship with my father. Further, I realize I had been psychologically abused my whole life. Drugs, pills, acting out, shopping—these were all responses to the bullet hole of pain these men caused, starting with my father. I certainly have my own issues with my mental health, but these relationships exacerbated them.

These relationships ended with mutually assured destruction. Although horrified by the abuse, I still struck back. I felt as if my cruel responses were self-defense. I hoped, if I was mean enough, they would get the picture and leave me alone forever. They didn't. They appeared to like the abuse, so they come back for more. Becoming the abuser made me sick to my stomach. It made me physically ill to cause these men pain, even though they had destroyed my life without missing a beat. Both David and Killian got very good versions of me. In both of those relationships, I had financial success, was at the top of my game careerwise, and was taking very good care of myself.

Both men found me on top and brought me to my knees, infecting my brain with brain weasels of self-doubt and destroying any self-esteem I ever had.

The person who probably wishes he never met me is Frank; he dated a rock-bottom drunk who spent money as if she were printing it. Frank dated a dumpster fire of a person and stayed loyal. David and Killian got a me as close to perfection as I ever was and treated me as if I were garbage. That brings levels of pain and embarrassment that, unless you've experienced it, you simply won't understand. Both relationships put me in the psych ward with trauma-bond withdrawals leaving me almost unable to function.

It was only after Killian that I realized how everything was intertwined—my issues, like the ADHD and bipolarity; their issues with narcissistic abuse; and the substance abuse. Each issue cannot be treated in isolation. They need to be treated with a holistic approach. The high and lows of narcissistic abuse amplifies a bipolar condition. The bipolarity causes me to self-medicate. The self-medication causes more narcissistic abuse. The escalating abuse causes PTSD. The PTSD escalates the substance abuse. On, and on…the conveyor belt of pain and pointlessness. That conveyor belt started in childhood; I just didn't realize it.

The only way to stop the insanity is to detox your entire life—not just your body, but your mind, your home, your friendships, and your family members with whom you are close. Your only hope of surviving this war is a commitment to peace and simplicity because, moving forward, that will make you extremely undesirable to narcissists; they love chaos and drama, even though they would never admit it. David and Killian brought chaos, drama, pain, money problems, and abuse into my life—all the things from my childhood I was trying to leave behind. A new simplicity to my life will repel their materialistic, superficial nature.

I can work on all this in the future; right now, my whole life is collapsing before my eyes, and I need to get a handle on it. Mutually assured destruction, it will be years before I'm in a good place again, if that ever happens. My two worst relationships were reenactments of my parents' marriage. Apparently, I have more issues than I thought. I'm leaving my own personal Vietnam, a second tour of duty, but I vow never to return. Just as a soldier finds when returning from war, you don't realize how bad it was until you try to reenter society. The emotional whiplash leaves you internally shaken to the point that you self-isolate into a nervous breakdown.

Dark Night of the Soul

Definition:
A term that goes back a long time. It is used to describe what one could call a collapse of a perceived meaning in life, an eruption into your life of a deep sense of meaninglessness. It is very close to what is conventionally called depression. A collapse of the whole conceptual framework for your life, the meaning that your mind had given it.

— *Eckhart Tolle*

Stage One—Initial Crisis

Christmas Day was the beginning of a shitstorm I didn't see coming. It was the coldest day in forty years, with temperatures far below zero, though there was very little snow on the ground. Upon awakening, I felt unusually cold, but headed to the bathroom to brush my teeth. Nothing came out of the spicket; I would soon discover that the pipes were frozen. So much for brushing my teeth. I ran downstairs to find the furnace, although still functioning, was not able to keep up with the frozen air assaulting the house from the outside. I was at a loss as to what to do— I began calling repairmen, but it was Christmas Day, a historically shitty day for me anyway.

I drove to Killian's and quickly told him what was going on. I was probably going to need a place to stay; however, he advised that he wasn't ready for a relationship. We had been seeing each other for over a year and half, but he still wasn't ready for a relationship. It was obvious that he wasn't lying in this regard. There was no Christmas present—not even a ten-dollar item—at his house for me. Either I didn't mean enough to him to warrant a present, or we had very different value systems. The reality was, if he couldn't financially afford a ten-dollar present for his girlfriend, he couldn't mentally afford a girlfriend on any level. Pissed beyond measure, I drove to my daughter's house to exchange presents.

I thought I had outdone myself on the presents, but not everyone agreed. The long history of shitty Christmases continued. Arriving home, I discovered that water was flooding my kitchen. I ran into the basement to shut off the water, only to discover that the ceiling in the basement had collapsed. This was a clusterfuck of colossal proportions.

This additional stress was more than I could take. There were delays with the publisher for my first book, I was still unable to find a steady-paying job due to the misdemeanors on my record, and now Killian and I were breaking up. Add to that the background anger over stagflation and the poor political climate, along with an ever-increasing lack of girlfriends with whom to vent, and I was reaching my breaking point.

* * *

Stage Two—Loss of Direction and Hope

While the relationship with Killian had already started to sour, he was part of my routine. In the span of twenty-four hours, I was forced to move into a hotel, as my house was uninhabitable, I lost my boyfriend, and I still had no job. I had even recently distanced myself from the girl-friends whom I knew from when I was still using. Without a boyfriend to motivate me, girlfriends to vent to, or money to get out of the house, and with all the background anger, I began to sink into a depression. Every facet of my routine had been upended. The further I sank into the depression, the worse my situation became. I was missing meals, ignoring my medication schedule, and no longer taking my mental health strolls around the neighborhood. I could no longer quilt in the hotel room, I lost interest in my writing career, and every attempt at applying for a job was met with a resounding no. The further the routines in my life slipped away, the deeper the depression—once unmedicated,

I began to lose my grip on reality, sanity, and hope. I began to malfunction on all levels. I knew what I needed to do— I needed professional help. I called 911 and asked to be taken the nearest "department of mental hygiene."

* * *

Stage Three—Emotional Rock Bottom

Hopefully, this will be the last time I ever get pink-slipped to a hospital because of a deteriorating mental state. Last thing I remember was being in my kitchen and having what seemed like a seizure. I was jerking involuntarily, unable to control my muscle movements, and screaming that Killian was coming to kill me. That he was hunting me down as a serial killer would. In the month leading up to the breakup, he did seem to give off a creepy serial-killer attitude, which was one of the many reasons for the breakup, but I was also unmedicated. I was no longer trusting my judgment, however, on anything. I was gaslighting myself.

I was somewhere in Youngstown, Ohio, in a "behavioral health clinic" for a nervous breakdown. I had been feeling the nervous breakdown coming on for months. So many events led up to the hospitalization—adjusting to living alone for the first time in my life, adjusting to sobriety, adjusting to unemployment, and adjusting to empty nesting. Plus, I'm going through a breakup.

This was, by far, the worst institution I had ever been in. I awoke on a cot—it can't even be called a bed. No blankets were allowed, and the pillow was plastic. One wall was painted pea green to break up the monotony of the room, but to no avail. The bathroom didn't have the kind of fixtures that you find in a home. The whole space was devoid of sharp objects, like screws or nails, that could be used to inflict harm on yourself or others. The windows had bars over them to prevent escape. The room heater vacillated between extreme heat and no heat at all. I looked over, and my roommate was retching into a garbage pail.

I had been burying my emotions for years. After an appointment with my therapist, I cried, really cried, for the first time in six years. Six long years since I was truly in touch with my emotions. In those six years, I had gotten divorced and sold the family home, my father had passed, and I got sober. I started a new job, moved away from my hometown, and went through two breakups. Both of my daughters got married, and I had a long-lost brother return to my life, the brother who had previously entered the witness protection program. I became an author, quit my part-time job, and lost more girlfriends than I can count right now. There were many positives and negatives, and the deconstruction of my external life was triggering a deconstruction internally. This time, though, I will make sure I reconstruct things in such a way that I never hit bottom again.

It was a very a tumultuous six years, and I never shed a tear until I felt on the inside that it was safe to give in to the tears. Once I started crying, I cried for three days straight, sobbing so uncontrollably that I couldn't get out of bed, feed myself, or even shower. The nervous breakdown, or breakthrough, was long overdue.

It's so disorienting to be institutionalized. I was given no more respect than a sock whose mate has been missing for months. The lack of respect was palpable. I wasn't given the respect a dog gives a tree. Anger and despair rushed in quickly. *How long will I be here? What about the people who are counting on me? Why did my daughters get the bad luck of having a mentally unstable mother.* Enveloped by shame and guilt, I was sober, so I couldn't drink the emotions away. *This too shall pass. It might pass like a kidney stone, but it will pass.*

I had obviously been given no medication as my brain was as clear as a bell. The lights were dimmed in an attempt to keep the patients sleepy and subdued—it clearly wasn't working. I could hear the screams of the other patients. Some had foul mouths, some were speaking incoherently, and some were just shrieking.

How did I get here? I don't mean just today; I mean when did my life take this severe and dramatic turn? I had graduated with honors when I earned a master's degree. I had climbed the French Alps. But in addiction, I'm either the king of the hill or in a trap house, and this felt like a trap-house situation. I was sober—I just needed to find my happy medium when I got out. My middle ground—living neither in poverty nor in excess. I was long overdue for a true, fundamental change in the way I lived my life. I couldn't keep doing what I had been doing. The lack of self-care, chasing money, clothes, and Killian, not ever making myself as high a priority as I needed to. *This place feels like a county jail. The hysterical patients, the aggressively obtuse nurses, the lack of supervision. My shit will get so straight when I get out. I am never getting locked up again.*

The anger continued to brew. I had clawed my way out of poverty. I had sacrificed for my education, my kids, my ex-husbands. And, still, this genetic time bomb had gone off, and I'd been discarded by society. I was being treated no better than clothes on their way to Goodwill. *No, when I get out, my shit will never be out of line again.* The last time I had been that determined was when I earned my master's degree. *And if my roommate tells me one more time she failed a drug screen because she ate poppy-seed bagels, I'm going to scream.*

***

Stage Four—Waking Up to the Truth

Lying there next to my roommate, who had the drug-riddled bagels, led me to examine myself on a deeper level. Through sobriety coaching and therapy, I was becoming aware of my issues and the baggage that I had picked up from unhealthy relationships, starting with my parents. My father always threw money at a problem instead of trying to solve it. Check—I do that too. It leads to rescuing-the-victim and people-pleasing tendencies. In active addiction, I was the perpetual victim, but would switch to a rescuing victim, and then a persecuting victim, depending on the situation. I had picked up bad relationship habits from my marriage to David, like abusive tendencies. The relationships with Frank and Killian were so short because of my sobriety. I couldn't stay sober with Frank, and with Killian, I was clearheaded enough to pull the plug as the red flags started flying.

It's impossible to escape the transfer of these bad habits sometimes. As with checking into a hotel with bed bugs, there is no chance of leaving unscathed. My mother and father had a rescuer-saver dynamic. That's odd—David, Frank, and Killian were all relationships with the rescuer-saver dynamic. All three of these men gave me less than the bare minimum in a relationship, just like my father. My adult relationships were simply reenactments of my parents' marriage. Ugh—that's a hard pill to swallow.

Was I easily going into relationships, or did I just not expect anything at all? Did I not expect anything because I didn't even know what I wanted? I called Killian every name in the book, but I myself am a walking red flag, at least right now. I had been avoiding commitment since that first kiss in sixth grade.

Although I hadn't taken a drink in three years, I hadn't yet achieved emotional sobriety. I hadn't fully grieved all that I had lost. I hadn't confronted the dark sides of my personality, as I was still on my pink cloud. I hadn't yet rightsized my ego and still hadn't overcome the shame of my downfall. The emotional cost of breaking generational cycles is far larger than I had anticipated, but I am still betting that it's worth it.

I was discharged from the hospital and returned home. Almost immediately, friends started showing up. But not to help—to continue to ask for favors. After informing them that I was in such bad shape that I could barely follow through on taking care of myself, they became angry and belligerent. I realized just how superficial and transactional these relationships really were. As I was hitting an emotional rock bottom, they just kept showing up with their hands out. Me, me, me—what about me? This rock bottom forced me to put an end to people-pleasing forever. I said no to more people and favors during this time than I had my whole life. Painful, but very necessary. I wasn't being difficult. I was now difficult to manipulate. There's a world of difference between the two.

Like the story of David and Goliath, it's the smallest of issues that brings me to my knees. But were they small issues? The unsuccessful search for gainful employment left me feeling no more valuable than chum in the water, and my mother's shadow was inescapable; but at least

I finally knew why—my relationships were merely reenactments of her marriage. She married a guy who had one foot out the door, and I involved myself with men who had one foot out the door. I'm not nearly as ready for a relationship as I thought. As Killian was smacking sunburns, it at least made me aware of what needed to be addressed and purged before this reconstruction.

***

Stage Five—Spiritual Study

As down on myself as I had been, I began to feel incredibly blessed. My sobriety stayed intact throughout this spiritual desolation and emotional bankruptcy. My home was warm and comfortable, and my daughters were top-notch kids. And I didn't lose all my friends, just the opportunistic ones. Quilting as a mindfulness activity was very satisfying and a great creative outlet. My volunteer work was my way of giving back to a planet that had given so much to me. Yes, I'm terrible at relationships, but I need to count my blessings more often. If I can't appreciate a coffee and a doughnut at rock bottom, why would the universe bless me with more than that?

My spirituality is still shaky, but I do find that I'm naturally aligned with Buddhist principles. Three years into sobriety, and I'm still taking it one day at a time. Rome wasn't built in a day, as they say. And the road to hell is paved with good intentions. I decided to enter a period of extended celibacy before I messed with any more heads, hearts, and souls. My problems haven't disappeared in sobriety; they have only revealed themselves, but at least I've stopped running long enough to address them.

On the plus side, my work ethic has improved by one thousand percent, my finances are falling into place, and my home has never been cleaner and more organized. Transfer addiction seems to be subsiding as I'm not shopping or overeating as if they were my job. This is nothing more than a run-of-the-mill nervous breakdown due to my nervous system being dysregulated for so long. The never-ending merry-go-round of fight-or-flight, freeze, and fawn led to fatigue and finally a near-catastrophic flop.

My life now is decluttering—after a lifetime of overaccumulating and overextending, my simplified life is more fulfilling and peaceful. Giving myself permission to rest is both necessary and important. Not every day has to count. Self-discipline has been cultivated to a degree that hadn't been there before; this has allowed me to realign my priorities and goals in life. When you're on an airplane, they instruct you to put the oxygen mask on yourself before putting it on others. I'm finally doing that because, when I don't, everything falls apart.

Drinking had drowned out my voice in my relationship with David. Even though I was no longer drinking, that toxic trait didn't simply disappear. During my drinking career, I was stuffing my feelings even further down—a recipe for disaster, to be sure. I was still learning to communicate my needs and boundaries. The relationship between David and me was death by a thousand paper cuts, and I was allowing that script to enter my other relationships as well. I was punished for being assertive, and I was punished for being agreeable. If I'm going to be punished regardless, I'd rather be punished for being assertive. Once I found my voice, I didn't let anyone silence it.

* * *

Stage Six—Authentic Living

Embracing my eccentricity is the only way to live in peace and alignment with myself. Embracing my identity comes with fewer problems than running from it. But I sensed I was overcorrecting. Going from extreme people-pleasing to no fucks given, from too impulsive to overly cautious, from overly agreeable to difficult, from party girl to nearly Amish. I'm still course correcting and trying to find the happy medium, but at least I'm self-aware enough to know what needs to be addressed. I'm self-disciplined enough to know where to direct my focus, motivated enough to act, mature enough to take accountability. Now, I'm focusing on genuine relationships.

It's been said that the opposite of addiction is connection, and addiction interferes with the connections that we desire. The three narcissistic men in my life conditioned me to hide my authenticity, the very best parts of me. Never again. Once I feel I can't be authentic around you, it's time to bounce permanently, and early on. At least with Killian I was able to recognize what was happening inside of seven months, instead of twenty-two years, as with David. Progress, not perfection. This isn't my first narcissistic rodeo, though. It'll be a good two years before I feel like myself again. But I won't ever be this version of myself again, and that's a good thing.

Hidey Up

Definition:
When you're supposed to tidy up your apartment, but you just hide the mess in your closet or bedroom.

Exemplification of Usage:
I'm supposed to have company here in twenty minutes. It's time to hidey up!

Life improved so dramatically after the great purge of cancerous relationships, so quickly, that I can't believe I waited this long. My fear of missing out was completely unwarranted. Sure, I didn't see friends as much, but when I did, I could remember all of it. Money didn't disappear, and I didn't have to worry about driving home. In fact, now that I could drive at any time of night or day without fear of driving drunk, I expanded my horizons. I went to social outings and events that I never would've considered in my drinking days.

Drinking as a coping skill didn't work for me. My new and resumed hobbies are now my healthy coping skills. My list of books to be read and craft projects not only provide a creative outlet, but also serve as art therapy. Drinking is just so normalized as the go-to solution for stress. Problem was, it created more stress than it eliminated. Being single is somehow looked down upon, but men brought me to my knees almost as badly as pills did. It's time to invest in myself to a degree that I haven't before.

Drinking, shopping, men had simply become part of my routine. Going to happy hour after work became standard procedure; I saw friends, and I had dinner. But these friends didn't really provide the support for which I was looking. They might be there if I wanted to vent about my boss, but would they be there when I needed a helping hand to move, would they be there if one of my brothers passed, or would they be there to cheer me on if I ever got my dream job? I suspected at the time it was a resounding no, and it turns out I was right. I spent years rationalizing all the ways that I was a normal drinker, and I spent time telling myself I just wasn't ready. Getting arrested scared me straight, and I haven't looked back since.

What I hadn't expected was improvements in my character when I wasn't even trying. My work ethic improved by one thousand percent. I was no longer ducking out of work to get to happy hour. I was staying on top of grading my papers because the preoccupation with drinking was gone. The amount of available time that appeared was incredible. Not just the time spent using, but the copious amount of time doing addiction calculus—counting my pills and dividing them by the amount of time they needed to last. Looking at my bank account and trying to stretch that money into more six-packs and nights out. Crawling around on the floor, hoping a pill had dropped, and treating it like Christmas morning if I found one that had rolled under the bed. The amount of headspace my addiction was occupying was much larger than I had previously realized. This headspace was now being put to good use elsewhere.

My finances improved, especially when I realized how easily transfer addiction could get ahold of me. I had started to overspend on clothes, home décor, or crafting supplies. I found apps on my phone that helped with all these issues. I had never felt I was a good housekeeper, but in my new-found time, my house became more organized than it had ever been. With my work ethic improved, my finances in order, and my home organized, I was feeling as if my shit had never been so straight in my life. The lack of chaos from mismanaged finances, disorganization, and misguided priorities reaped additional rewards as well. My stress levels were the lowest they ever had been—well, at least since my twenties. There was no need to drink to alleviate stress, as I was addressing my stressors instead of avoiding them.

I felt very overstimulated in early sobriety. I had dulled my senses for so long that the world seemed very intense suddenly. Lights were too bright, noises too loud. I had to readjust locations I might frequent to avoid that overstimulation, and I perfected the Irish goodbye. My vacation to Gatlinburg was a prime example. I had not expected it to be so overstimulating—neon signs, endless shopping opportunities, and the advertisements for moonshine were ubiquitous. Vacationing remains the largest sobriety challenge, as vacationing was my first "no rules" drinking. I found I needed to mentally prepare more than I realized for a vacation.

My mental state didn't fully recalibrate until three years into sobriety—now I understood why medical diagnoses in early sobriety are notoriously unreliable. My brain was still adjusting to the pickle juice being gone. I had fully surrendered, realizing that I was a cucumber that had been turned into a pickle, and there was no chance of ever being a cucumber again.

A series of epiphanies about myself kept rolling into my self-awareness. I had been a stranger to myself most of my life, and much of my personality was filled with poor coping mechanisms and trauma responses during active addiction. The self-awareness that I had gained when working with Joe, my sobriety coach, was the tip of the iceberg. These were the strengths and weakness in my personality. That self-awareness was limited, as it didn't address some larger core issues related to my one-sided friendships, unsuccessful relationships, and lack of both solid communication and conflict-resolution skills. I was unaware of my invisible disabilities, and so couldn't accommodate them. I was fully unaware that I was living out my parents' marriage in every relationship I had, accepting the absolute bare minimum from men as my mom had done with my dad.

All this missing time triggered, once again, the five stages of grief. And the only way to get through it is, well, to get through it. I had been avoiding my emotions, my issues, and my addictive tendencies my entire life. The more I avoided them, the more they snowballed into larger problems. There was nothing I could do but mourn the time I had lost. Time can never be retrieved. But this realization inspired a recommitment to never take time for granted again. It is my most valuable resource.

I had to let go of the resentments toward David. Yes, I had paid his way through the police academy, going so far as to pay his child support and alimony to his first wife—a stupid move that I hope no one else ever makes—only to be turned out like a stray cat, but the divorce provided the biggest glow up I had ever experienced. The scorched earth that my life had once been provided the most fertile soil I ever had for a new life.

I had a new appreciation for the little things in life—food, water, sleep, and shelter. Once you are stuffed twenty-girls deep in a halfway house without these essentials, that will happen. But if I didn't appreciate the ginger ale and hot dog at rock bottom, why would I appreciate the blessings at the top?

My net health has never been higher—physically, mentally, and financially. Without a positive net health, my net wealth would never improve. The vast oscillations of success, fortune, and health in my life had to stop. I don't have another substance-abuse recovery in me, but I also don't have another romantic recovery in me, or another financial recovery. I'm fifty-three, after all, and the rubber band of my psychological resilience has already been stretched out one too many times. It can only be stretched out so many times before permanent burnout sets in.

The ADHD tax issues seemed to be resolving, or at least lessening. With my newfound organizational skills, I wasn't buying items I had lost, for instance. I was focusing on life skills for which I never had the foundation. As with a house, if a foundation is bad, it's only a matter of time before everything falls apart. Though the breakup with Killian was the worst yet, it also provided therapy breakthroughs that probably wouldn't have happened otherwise. The positive momentum is picking up speed; I can feel it. I'm building an empire with no boyfriend, no solid friendships, in sight. It's in this period of struggle that my core values are being solidified. In this period of struggle, my resilience is strengthened. In this period of struggle, I experience a tremendous amount of growth in a short period of time. I will come to realize later that the beauty of my success was in the struggle all along.

Getting sober was just the beginning. I hadn't yet turned a flashlight to my own issues that I was running from.

By the end of the dark night of the soul and the subsequent ascension flu, I finally had the foundation I needed. I finally had changed my self-sabotaging money habits, cutting so many corners; all that was left was a circle. I had improved my executive-function skills and developed routines. I was now ready for all the blessings the universe had in store for me.

Panic Economics

Definition:
When the economy is driven by fear, whether of a hurricane, ice storm, or wildfire; can also be political.

Exemplification of usage:
Her: I heard guns are flying off the shelf. Everyone is convinced they're getting taken away after yesterday's shooting.

Me: Your guns aren't going anywhere; it's in the Constitution. It's just panic economics.

Her: You're right. Almost like Y2K all over again.

A hazard of living one day at a time is that it's entirely possible to be "too" present. In terms of my finances, I never looked ahead *enough*. The only way I was going to able to pursue my plans effectively was to reduce my money stress, which appears paradoxical. However, if you are living in a foreshortened future, which many trauma survivors do, you have a hard time even imagining where you'll be forty-five days out, let alone worry about finances.

Our news cycle and economic climate does us no favors in this regard. Since I was a child, the news has been trying to scare us into poverty—that's a bold statement, I know, but scared people spend money more impulsively than a calmer person would. Think of when the pandemic started. The rush on toilet paper is a prime example. Frank bought all kinds of things in preparation for a societal collapse. Starting with the 1970s, we've had killer bees, the gangs of Los Angeles, Y2K, the Cold War, radon, and the list goes on and on about imminent societal collapse, looting, and food shortages that spur us to spend money. Combine that with my addictive personality and a shaky foundation dating back to childhood—no wonder I have money problems.

The self-awareness of my invisible disabilities greatly helped me get my finances in check. The most expensive of my challenges is my ADHD. This affliction has led to more lost money than I can count, and I'm not even speaking of the fact that people with ADHD are more likely to struggle with addiction. The disorganization, varying energy levels, and impact on my quality of life is very expensive. If you've ever had a surgery that requires pain medication afterwards, you've likely been told to stay ahead of the pain. By the same token, the best time to work on your health and finances is when times are good. This was a large mindset shift for me, having had both a childhood and a marriage that kept me operating from crisis to crisis. My nervous system was dysregulated; simply focusing on getting out of fight-or-flight mode had an enormous impact on my quality of life.

Your nervous system can shift from fight-or-flight to fawn, freeze, fatigue, and eventually flop. I've flopped—had a nervous breakdown—five times in my life. I've got to keep shit so straight that I never flop again. It requires too much to come back from, and that's only one of the problems involved. I call the fawning response the indentured servant of my personality. Out of habit, I will wait on a partner or my children hand and foot. It's a little *too* obsequious. Inadvertently, I can fawn over other people at my own expense. It's often seen as a people-pleasing response. Not only did I see the other women in my life do this, but fawning keeps the peace in an abusive relationship, further cementing this dysfunctional habit. My freeze response, which is like a deer-in-the-headlights type of response, will cause me to be preoccupied with receiving a text back or wondering what the other person is thinking. The constant merry-go-round of fight-or-flight, fawn, and freeze will dysregulate anyone to the point of fatigue or flop.

This dysregulation will affect your relationships, your spending habits, and your career. Putting your health first will provide limitless benefits. Once I left the permanently dysregulated state, I could focus on getting my health in order. The ADHD, for example, led to lost items, which

I had to repurchase. The ADHD also led to dopamine seeking, which manifests itself in shopping, drinking, and gambling. It also led to background anger, which bubbles over at the most inopportune moments. Reaching a more Zen state of mind allowed many other pieces to fall into place.

Flight mode will trigger workaholic tendencies, overthinking, anxiety issues, perfectionism, avoidance, hyperactivity, and loneliness. Fight mode will trigger bullying tendencies, explosive outbursts, irritability, self-harming behaviors, irritability, and judgmental attitudes. Freeze mode will make you indecisive, exhausted, and will cause you to isolate, dissociate, and desire to feel numb. Fawning is people-pleasing, feeling overwhelmed, exhibiting a lack of boundaries, being codependent, being self-critical, feeling as if you are losing your identity, and being unable to say no to everyone but yourself. The never-ending cycle leads to fatigue and eventually a nervous breakdown or flop. Having had the supervision of a feral cat as a child, two narcissistic relationships, and a few jobs that worked me to the point of exhaustion and treated me no better than a serf in the Middle Ages, I had been on this merry-go-round most of my life.

Sobriety is more than abstaining from your addiction of choice. It's emotional sobriety. It's calling yourself on your own bullshit. It's admitting you've had enough of your own dysfunction, and it's a commitment to end it.

What is emotional sobriety? Loving yourself enough to not sabotage your success. Loving yourself enough to not seek external validation in the latest designer purse or fancy vacation. Sure, these things can be nice, but what is the motivation behind them? Transferring my addiction from pills and alcohol to shopping, to people-pleasing, was not emotional sobriety. Fawning over men who couldn't care less if I lived or died caused me to reexamine my issues, which were apparently larger than I thought. I felt I loved my children and the men in my life unconditionally, but I couldn't love myself unconditionally. My father inadvertently taught me to throw money at problems, and in relationships, that comes off as trying to buy someone's love.

Emotional sobriety, for me, means an end to panic economics. No junk spending, impulsive shopping, or credit cards. If I don't have the money this week, I likely won't have it next week. I kept creating problems for future Susan to deal with, sabotaging my success before it arrived. Having put my money stress in check, I was relaxed enough to write poetry, enjoy my children, and chill the hell out while watching Netflix occasionally. Once I stopped over-consuming, I could tell this respect-the-hustle culture to get lost. Emotional sobriety was redefining my values. Instead of wanting more out of life, I wanted less, and to appreciate to a larger extent what I did have. I wanted to stop taking what I did have for granted and to give back to a world that had given so much to me.

I began to give back by volunteering at a local non-profit. As quilting had become my favorite hobby du jour, I began making specialty quilts that could be auctioned off at fundraising events. Volunteering got me out of the house for free and gave me the opportunity to make new friends. After the breakup with Killian, I isolated to a level that I never had before; it wasn't good for my sobriety. Sober breakups suck—I give that experience zero stars! Speaking from experience, don't get into a relationship if you don't think you can handle the fallout. I don't have another alcohol recovery in me, but I also don't have another financial or romantic recovery in me.

For the time being, I have to direct all the love I have to give toward me, and it seems to be paying off. I'm starting to feel as if that bullet hole of pain is almost gone. The void I was trying to fill has disappeared. And it disappeared with the absence of alcohol, men, and shopping. The void filled when my character issues were addressed. The void disappeared as I expressed gratitude for my home, food, and clothing. The void disappeared when I began quilting to volunteer my time. The void filled when I did nothing flashy or superficial. The void filled because I stopped running, chasing, and suppressing. The void filled because now I'm at peace after a lifetime of war.

Procrasti-dating

Definition:
Putting off dating simply because you like being single too much.

Exemplification of Usage:
I've been divorced for six years already. What started as taking a break turned into procrasti-dating.

Dating in 2023 is about as healthy as the Cuyahoga River when it was on fire, but even that river will recover sooner than the dating scene. In all seriousness, I've come across these six situations on the dating scene: the guy who is not ready for a relationship but will treat you as if you were his wife; the guy who brings a U-Haul to the third date; the guy who either is not over his ex or is still with his ex, but is already looking; the love-bombing ghoster; the guy who is not even in your league, but will still play you; and then the guy who is a mixed bag of disasters, a Y-chromosome potpourri of sorts.

Dating sober is a totally different ball game. There are things that I let slide in previous relationships that I won't let slide now. Being sober generally means that your memory is going to be intact, so if you're accused of making issues up, for instance, you can fall back on your memory, which was previously unreliable. It also means that you can hold yourself accountable to a level that you never have before, which increases your chances of a successful relationship. It's been said that an addict's emotional maturity is stuck at the age of their first drink, or even at the age of a particular trauma. In sobriety, your emotional maturity will increase. It's possible that thirteen-year-old Sue had been showing up in my relationships all along, which means those relationships never had a fighting chance. Rescuing-victim Sue had also shown up previously. Now, I look for a partner, not a project. People tend to date to their level of self-esteem and unresolved trauma. Two people, who seem completely mismatched on the outside, can be nearly identical internally.

Killian was the "not ready for a relationship" boyfriend who would say to your face that the relationship wasn't serious, but at the same time, we were together four out of the seven days of the week; we took three vacations together; and we did more socializing together than I had with anyone else with whom I had been involved, except David. I even accompanied Killian to funerals and on one occasion to a court date. But, yeah, it was a nothing-serious relationship. Truthfully, I agreed that he wasn't ready for a relationship. His personal life was a stream of crises, and he didn't even show up for his own life. So how could he show up for mine? Killian also brought into a relationship a level of mind games that I had never experienced. Such as saying that we weren't serious but acting as husband and wife. His actions didn't align with his words, which, in my opinion, shows a lack of integrity. But if you're not ready for a relationship, stay completely out of the dating pool.

Oddly, the guys who don't want a relationship seem to be the most pissed when you stop dating them. I'm not sure what else they expect to happen. That I would hang out in the relationship waiting room for seven years? I'm already embarrassed that I did it for seven months. The dating scene provides mixed messages—being strung along, not only being given the bare minimum, but also being asked to appreciate the little you are given. The whole experience gets zero stars, in my opinion. It was an even bigger waste of time than active addiction. These guys don't want a relationship, but also don't want to leave you alone. That's going to be a hard pass for me.

Frank was a great example of the guy who brings a U-Haul to the third date. We met on election night in 2017, he said "I love you" the very first weekend, and he was moved in within two weeks of first meeting him. Six weeks in, we were engaged. He's the opposite of the "not ready for a relationship" guy—this guy wants a relationship to show up faster than a Happy Meal. Like a Happy Meal, this relationship won't be very satisfying either. The U-Haul shows up in more ways than one. The emotional baggage in the U-Haul starts showing itself very early in the relationship.

The personal issues with which each person is dealing take over the relationship before you can even enjoy the courtship. Frank and I were nothing more than drinking buddies by about three months in.

But of all my relationships, I appreciate Frank the most. His no-rules drinking policy accelerated my alcoholism so fast that I was nearly dead five months in. My addiction was going to accelerate to this level at some point; Frank just helped it happen in record time and saved me a few years of "on the fence" drinking. Frank was a genuinely nice guy—if my car broke down, he was there; if I had a court date, he was there; if I wanted to stay up and talk, he was there. Our health problems interfered right out of the gate, though. It's almost impossible to have a healthy relationship with someone who doesn't even have a healthy relationship with themselves.

Then there is the "not over my ex" guy or, worse yet, the "I've decided to get a divorce; she just doesn't know it" guy. He'll try to convince you he's over his ex, even though they are still living together. Side chicks never win; bow out of this situation immediately. These guys are like monkeys—they don't want to let go of the branch they are on until they find a new branch. This describes David and me. The stress of David's divorce took over the relationship almost immediately. Killian was also not over his ex. Relationships with these guys feel like unpaid therapy, not dating. Ideally, you want the courtship to last as long as possible. As David and I dated during his divorce, he was pissed off much of the time very early on. With Killian, I just never felt I was going to live up to his ex, or, worse yet, I was paying for her mistakes. Again, zero stars. These guys' need for therapy is transferred to you by osmosis. The fact you even gave these guys a chance is a good indicator that you needed therapy before you even started on the dating scene. You'll know so much about their ex, you'll feel the need to contact her to see how she's doing. Is your mom okay? Did you get that promotion? I wasn't that bad, but you get the point. There will be no room for you in the relationship.

The love-bombing ghoster—he's a combination of the first two types. He starts off strong. He's attentive, takes you on dates, says all the right things, and then, three weeks in, disappears. He apparently lacks the communication skills to tell you what's going on. He's an efficient one, so this disappearing act will happen early on. Mine showed up when I was already suffering from dating fatigue, so it was no skin off my back. In fact, if his communication skills were that bad, it was a blessing in disguise. It's possible he sensed my dating fatigue, and it was a deal-breaker for him. I'll never know. I know I have deal-breakers, and I'm not everyone's cup of tea, but that's my best quality. I never wanted to be the town bicycle. I've always stayed true to myself in relationships, which is a very good thing.

The "not in your league" guy will embarrass you to a point that you've never been embarrassed before. For me, this was the dognapper. Of course, he wasn't a dognapper when we met; he was an English Lit major. For most girls, this is a guy from high school. You decide to give this guy a chance against your better judgment. This is the guy you date, and he self-destructs almost immediately after you make the relationship official.

Dating down isn't about finances; it's about character, integrity, and many other factors. It's about dating someone who has unresolved issues, doesn't have their shit together, or has different values. I know many women who think dating down will give them a guy who will treat them like a princess, one who will be so happy to have you that he will treat you better than you ever have been. I have found the opposite to be true. You will be treated worse than you ever have in your life; you will find yourself disrespecting yourself and your boundaries.

The mixed bag of disasters I found on the dating apps:

Is a racist.

Picks pointless arguments.

Is a miser.

Puts in low effort, often because he has no money. If he can't afford to buy you a meal or a ten-dollar Christmas gift, he not only can't financially afford you, but he can't mentally afford you.

Lives with his mom.

Makes fun of your lipstick.

Tells you that you are a giant bag of issues because you don't drink.

Killian was far and away the most painful breakup I've ever been through. We had the best physical relationship I've ever had; the conversations were stimulating and deep, and the chemistry was off the charts. The chemistry was the biggest red flag of them all. I've said it before, and I'll say it again—red-hot chemistry is merely a sign that your dysfunctions line up. For Killian and me, my people-pleasing lined up with his excessive need for control. That red-hot chemistry will turn, just as it did for David and me. With both men, I spent too much time trying to get them to treat me better, instead of just walking away. I spent too much time accepting the bare minimum. I didn't miss the red flags; they just felt like home. Both were so much like my father that it was creepy after a while. Killian's "one foot out the door" method to relationships mimicked my father's approach to his relationship with my mother. Their bare-minimum style was the same as my father's. Neither were even my type; they were just my pattern.

These two relationships were merely reenactments of my parents' marriage; clearly, I have some issues to clean up as well. My Electra complex came screaming through in both relationships; neither man even appeared to like women. I often wonder why either even tried to be in relationships at all, unless it was a status symbol of some sort.

I began to wonder why *I* even tried to be in a relationship since I have such strong loner tendencies. Right now, I'm off the market indefinitely. The cost-benefit ratio of a relationship isn't positive, and I've obviously done my fair share of damage as well. I miss the emotional support of a relationship—sitting down to a nice meal that I've cooked and having someone to spot me a fifty if I hit a rough patch—and then I remind myself that I've never even had that. If my last love was the guy who never even wanted me in the first place, Killian, I'll be pissed. It may be a self-fulfilling prophecy; he hurt me badly enough that it'll be hard to let my guard down again. Then I remember that I was in rehab for the first time at fourteen, so maybe this isn't my biggest issue.

Credit Crack

Definition:
*Being so addicted to credit cards that you
lose sight of the fact that you actually have
to pay it back.*

Exemplification of Usage:
*Her: Ever since my credit score improved,
I've applied for credit cards like crazy. It'll
take a couple of years to get back on track!*

Them: It's credit crack! So addicting!

Wherever you go, you take yourself with you. After
losing nearly a decade to addiction, I finally surrendered.
I began my recovery journey and ditched the booze and
the pills. Not surprisingly, this threw my body into a state
of shock. Post-acute withdrawal symptoms were felt by
my body for nearly a year after my last pill; that's probably
the reason people are advised not to make any big decisions during the first year of recovery. My body was still

craving dopamine hits it had become conditioned to the artificial highs of my drug habit. I suddenly was craving sugar, my shopping addiction came back full force, and I was suddenly spending too much time on social media. What was happening? Transfer addiction.

Although I was saving money hand over fist, I decided to try to rebuild my credit. I opened up several credit cards, thinking that because I was sober, I would suddenly be more responsible with money. During periods of mild depression and melancholy, I started shopping. I bought far too many clothes. More clothes than I would ever need. I overinvested in my hobbies of reading, scrapbooking, and quilting. I decided to buy high-end artwork for my home. And within a year, I had enough debt that I didn't know what to do. I finally realized I wasn't fully sober yet—I didn't have emotional sobriety, as I was still getting artificial dopamine hits from external sources like shopping and social media. The two fed off each other; every time I went time online, I was bombarded with buy, buy, buy! Consume more, worry less!

This was all occurring during my pink-cloud phase of recovery—the honeymoon period of recovery when everything is sunshine and rainbows. It felt as if nothing would ever go wrong in my life again because, well, I was sober. Addiction was ninety-nine of my one hundred problems, and I had solved my addiction. However, the way life works is that when one problem is solved, another—sometimes two or three—shows up in its place. Life will never be free of problems.

I cut up my credit cards, deciding that if I didn't have the money today, I wouldn't have the money in two months. I had been paying for items with credit, thinking that magically in two months all my finances would be in order, even though there was no evidence to support this notion.

Once again, I surrendered. Surrendering is the only way to win in a situation like this. Fighting it caused more problems. Waging a war on my problems only ever created more problems. The more I fought to control any of my circumstances, the more life showed me that I had no control over anything but me. Accepting defeat allowed me to win. I needed to pick my battles. I'm in my fifties now, and I don't have the same energy levels that I used to. Fighting every battle that comes my way will leave me too tired for the battles that really matter. I needed to save my energy for the important stuff, such as rebuilding my career, cleaning my house, doing my volunteer work, and the like. Fighting my addictive nature was a battle I was going to lose. All I could do was accept that I had never used credit cards appropriately in my life, and I probably never will; just as I had never met a pill I didn't like, I barely have ever met a store at the mall I didn't like.

Frustrated by my financial incompetence, I had to reframe the way I looked at shopping to stop the madness.

I began reading articles on how fast fashion is destroying the environment. I began noticing how very few items of clothes that I own have either the quality that I am looking for or the staying power I should expect for the money I was putting out. I began to look at my clothes on a cost-per-use basis. If I spent $100 on a nice outfit, and I only wore it five times, I was effectively spending $20 per use of that outfit. This became a very effective way of looking at my finances. If I spent $200 on making an heirloom quilt, this was more justifiable, as the heirloom quilt will be around for twenty-plus years, but the $100 outfit will be out of style in less than a year. Instead of trying to save money after I went on a spending spree, I decided to spend only the money that was left after I paid my bills and saved some money. I fundamentally changed the way I looked at money.

I also looked at my expenses as recurring and nonrecurring. Examining my finances, I had made purchases that were nonrecurring, like my living room furniture. In fact, it's quite possible, at my age, that this is the last furniture I will buy. The artwork, too, was nonrecurring. A house only needs so many decorations. But given the nature of fashion, it is a recurring expense. There will always be a new look sold in stores—it's unavoidable. The only way to win is to not play. Any money that I spend on fast fashion decreases the amount of money I have in the bank for incidentals. Incidentals are those unexpected expenses, such as the battery in your car dying or a new set of tires and brakes as your car ages. The pursuit of fast fashion, then, was putting the maintenance of my car at risk. When viewed through this lens, the leggings and sweaters were now costing me far more than $100. They were costing me peace of mind—in an emergency I might not have the money to keep my car running, which in turn could affect my career. The evidence was piling up fast that my shopping habit was costing me more than I realized.

The further into recovery I was, the more I noticed I was policing myself, and in some ways overcorrecting in the areas that I felt I needed to improve. Once a people-pleaser, I swung in the other direction to a "no fucks given" approach. Once overly impulsive, I was now proceeding with so much caution it could be debilitating at times. Once lacking any type of boundaries, I now cut people off without warning for crossing a boundary they didn't even know existed. I've always struggled to find balance, and the pendulum was swinging too far in the other direction. Once overly needy, I was now exhibiting hyper-independence. I went from being a party girl to a life so wholesome I felt puritanical.

With the elimination of drugs, alcohol, shopping, and doom scrolling online, I had a lot of time on my hands once again. I was still trying to regulate my nervous system naturally. Hiking, yoga, and quilting were all tools that I used to provide the endorphins my body was looking for in the absence of artificial dopamine. They were all activities that were allowing me to feel my emotions and release them in a nondestructive way. In sobriety, you get all your feelings back. This is a curse before it becomes a blessing. The heavy, negative emotions need to be cleared out to make way for contentment, peace, and joy.

All emotions serve a purpose. I went to great lengths to avoid any uncomfortable emotions, or even any decisions that went with those uncomfortable emotions. But avoiding them does no good. In fact, avoiding them only compounded the intensity of the problem and the associated fallout from the avoidance.

Throughout human history, many emotions have given rise to solutions. In my boredom, I felt the most creative. In my anger, I searched for solutions. In my excitement, I searched for friends and family to share the joy. The boredom of early sobriety became the most beneficial emotion to embrace. This boredom gave rise to a writing career and a quilting hobby. The boredom led to action, and those actions produced articles, books, stories, and heirlooms of which I can be proud. This boredom eventually gave way to pride. Once I embraced the negative, the positive began showing up. The only way to get through a forest is to, well, get through it. The only way to get through boredom, melancholy, and anger is to, well, get through them. But those emotions fade and change with time.

Once cleared out and purged, the heaviness of those emotions was gone, and I was free to feel happy, excited, and proud of my accomplishments. Fighting the emotions, just as I fought my addictions, was the wrong approach.

Radical acceptance was the better approach for me. The more fighting, the more conflict. The more I surrendered, the more peace I felt. I was accidentally improving myself and addressing my shaky foundation through trial and error. Oddly, the more I embraced my imperfections, the more confident I felt. Maybe I'll always be a walking contradiction, but at least I'm a happy contradiction, and that's a win I can live with.

The true cost of my addictive personality was revealing itself. Besides the drinking and drugging, the people-pleasing led to toxic relationships. The credit-card issue was compromising my future by giving future Susan not enough money to prepare for the essentials like home repair and car maintenance. The overall toxic nature I was exhibiting while addicted was straining relationships with family. Being in a state of perpetual crisis left me no time to look for a good job and feeling as if the crisis friend affected my self-esteem. My addiction was affecting every aspect of my life.

I saw more improvement in a few years of not drinking than in a decade of addiction. That should be all the motivation you need to start surrendering to your addictions. I'm not saying it's easy, but I am saying it's worth it.

The Joy of Missing Out

I've undergone a complete and total transformation as a person. There's no going back to the person I was before the addiction, and why would I want to? I have something I've never had before—inner peace, an appreciation of my own company, and healthy coping skills. I have so many things that money cannot buy—integrity, solid core values—and I'm no longer restless, irritable, and discontent. I now have the confidence that I can weather any storm and play whatever cards life deals me, good and bad. I've cultivated a support system, self-care routines, and I'm happy to report that I'm no longer a doormat that keeps the peace at my own expense. I have a healthy sense of self and a sense of pride that I've never had before. I'm able to be present for my children and friends, and I'm not cutting corners on any aspect of my life. I've finally developed the work ethic I never learned as a child, developed a financial literacy I never had, and have a strong desire to give back to a world that has given so much to me. I've learned to shift priorities as needed and to not care that I may disappoint others, as I would rather disappoint others than disappoint myself. I can't be all things to all people, and I will only self-destruct if I try.

I now have a dream job that I love. I can now fall back on those core strengths that were identified in my first character assessment, the ones that were the foundation for developing healthy coping mechanisms in early sobriety. I've been undoing so much societal conditioning, rejecting the respect-the-hustle culture to avoid burnout, ignoring hateful comments, and accepting constructive criticism. I have a sense of gratitude and humility that I never had before, and I realize that under different circumstances I could be living in a tent city somewhere. I can now give myself grace for my imperfections and not internalize any insults from people who don't even like themselves. I'm comfortable in my own skin, and I know that I'm not everyone's cup of tea, but, quite frankly, that's my best quality.

I was convinced that I couldn't live without alcohol and pills. They were my safety net against insomnia, stressful times, and a pick-me-up on my bad days. I used them to take the edge off, but they were the source of the rough edges in my life. I can sleep like a baby with the knowledge that people trust me now; I'm not running a scam on anybody or hiding activities from my family and law enforcement. I'm no longer robbing from Peter to pay Paul, and I've cultivated a life from which I don't need to escape.

Every day is a vacation when you break free from your addiction and live the life of your dreams. When I started to look at life as a blessing, even the trying times and difficulties started to feel like blessings. I get to go to work; I get to clean my house; I get to work on the flower beds. When my triggers were addressed head-on, more sparkle days showed up. When I started being grateful for the fact that I even had sparkle days to begin with, they all became sparkle days, with few exceptions.

After a lifetime of accumulation, I started decluttering my life, and I mean every aspect of my life. I let go of the feeling that I'm not good enough, I let go of the skinny shaming, and I let go of every expectation that had been placed on me. I let go of materialism and chasing the fun. I decluttered my entire existence, letting go of toxic friends, clothes that I'll never wear, and a never-ending to-do list. Once I focused on my net health, the more my net wealth increased, and not in the monetary sense.

Oddly, the more I let go, the more everything I ever wanted showed up. As I released greed, money showed up. As I released pain, joy showed up. As I decluttered my house, the clutter in my brain disappeared. As I was about to throw in the towel on my dream job, a headhunter showed up. As I shifted my financial priorities to accumulating experiences rather than stuff, I developed memories to last a lifetime. The more I let go of any sense of control, the more abundant my life became. When I stopped finding fault with myself, I stopped finding faults in others. The more I learned to embrace the suck, the more the suck disappeared. As my net health increased, my nonmonetary wealth increased exponentially.

The fear of missing out? More like the joy of missing out! Missing out on hangovers, dramatic fights, and shaky hands. Missing out on the judgmental looks from others and my constant self-criticism. What I've found is copious amounts of time, energy, and loving people. What I've found is worth every excruciatingly embarrassing moment of my past, from the illegal activities to the trips to the hospital where the doors only go one way. I would go through all of it, all over again, to get to where I am now.

What I have now cannot be purchased with all the money in the world, and what I have now nobody can take away from me. What I have now is worth everything I've lost, and I'm holding on to it for dear life. I live a life of no regrets and a sense that the bad days will not stay, because I won't let them. I continue to live life on life's terms, but I'll do it stone-cold sober, remembering—nay, savoring—every detail for years to come. It's a beautiful life that feels as if it is only just beginning at the age of fifty-two. My long-awaited second peak is here, and I'm enjoying every single minute of it!

Please Don't Question My Smile

Almost a couple of years have gone by
Since you've seen me.
I know it's been quite a while.
I don't get to hold you anymore, don't want you no more,
But please don't question my smile…

I'm so free without you,
a couple of years gone by.
I wake up without you, don't think about you.
I wake up to the songs of the birds
Instead of shaky hands
And you controlling my mind.

I count the sunsets
With the time that has gone by.
I get to live in awe now,
Dance, breathe freely as I live life without you.
Please don't question my smile.

Why am I thinking about you
With all this time gone by?
Just counting my blessings
And grateful I don't need you anymore.

It was time to say goodbye.
I just wanted you for a night—once in a while.
You want to hang on forever.
My smile didn't reach my eyes—wait, did I smile?

So now I'm without you and don't question my smile.
It was time to say goodbye for too long now.
You're no longer my style.

When we get together,
I'm not sure where we're sleeping,
But they are not memories worth keeping…
I hate memories that stay for a while.

You ruined a young girl who never figured out her dreams.
That's why it was so easy to keep her
When she only wanted you once in a while, not forever.
That's how you took ahold of her; you preyed on her smile.
It's been time to say goodbye for too long now
Because you're cramping my style…

When we get together, I forget my pain for a while.
But now I think about it, pain is your style.
It's time to say goodbye now.
I'm not in need of forgotten memories;
/ that is no longer my style.
So please don't question my smile.

Vacation Cookware

Definition:
Whatever low-budget dishes you use when you are on vacation. Anywhere from camping equipment to just convenient cookware—who wants to wash dishes on vacation?

Exemplification of usage:
I can't wait to use a real fork again. This vacation cookware is wearing on my nerves—I never liked plastic utensils.

It's the fall of 2023, and I'm living a life on vacation from my addiction. Free from the obsession of drinking and drugging. One of financial freedom as well. I'm in a wonderful, loving, romantic relationship, I have two beautiful, successful daughters. I've accomplished everything I ever set out to do in this life, even after losing a decade to addiction. I reconnected with a girlfriend from high school. We lamented over boy troubles on our local staycation. I was launching my TikTok and wanted to highlight sober fun around town. I needed to get all men off my mind for a while; coincidentally, this girlfriend was having men troubles too. Our reconnection was perfect timing.

The *Merriam-Webster Dictionary* defines a staycation as "a vacation spent at home or nearby." The benefits of a staycation are that you get all the reinvigorating effects of a vacation in a fraction of the time and cost. Between hyperinflation, kids' activities, and the crisis at the nation's airports, staycations should be on the rise.

I have been staycationing in my hometown of Cleveland all summer, and I hope that you will either want to visit the reinvented mistake on the lake or, at the very least, that you will staycation in your own hometown. Amateur scientists and *Ancient Alien* fans love to daydream about going to outer space when they haven't even explored their own backyards. I decided to explore my own backyard, and I suggest that you do the same.

Cleveland, Ohio, is located on Lake Erie, the smallest of the Five Great Lakes. Its location has mostly been a curse— the Cuyahoga River and the canal made it a perfect location for manufacturing, but the factories almost brought about its demise. The Industrial Revolution was both a bane and a boon. But Cleveland has been back on the rise for quite some time. I have had the most affordable fun of my life this summer! Fun that is good for the whole family.

My first stop on my staycation was the Superelectric Pinball Parlor on the west side of Cleveland, located at 6500 Detroit Avenue, on the border of Lakewood, Ohio. The cost of play is six dollars per person for the day! The pinball machines are clean and well-maintained, and they make your inner child happy with a heavy dose of nostalgia. There is a cocktail bar for adults, but it doesn't serve food. You will have to go elsewhere for dinner. My date and I went to the Ninja City Kitchen and were not disappointed.

Swings-N-Things in North Olmsted was another stop this summer. It is an entertainment hub with arcade games, Putt-Putt golf, go-carts, batting cages, and more. It was $40 a person for unlimited play for the day. The arcade games were extra, but it was still a hell of a bargain. I had never been on a go-cart before—I found it very exhilarating! I even had a homemade ice-cream cone, and I won the round of Putt-Putt that I played.

The Rock & Roll Hall of Fame and museum was the highlight of the staycation! It currently has a Beatles exhibit, which was great fun to watch…and talk about nostalgic! The cost of the exhibit was $35 per person. I would reserve at least two hours for this trip as it will take that long just for a cursory walk through it. The most unpleasant part of the experience was the gift shop—I was excited to buy souvenirs, but they didn't take cash. Unfortunately, I did not get a Rock Hall T-shirt as a result.

This is a just a quick glance at the fun I had this summer, and this is only the first in a series of staycation-fun travels. I have noticed an increase in my motivation, a decrease in my burnout, and an increase in my overall happiness as a result of my staycationing. The ever-elusive work-life balance has come into focus by exploring my own backyard.

More importantly, I'm on vacation from my addiction. There are no more morning shakes, no hangovers, no distressing rides home from the bar. In recovery, it was easier to identify the covert abuse by Killian and to end the relationship early, as I wasn't letting anything slide anymore. The elimination of my credit cards provided more financial freedom than I could've ever imagined.

My life is falling into place. Abstinence is just the first step. I have to address the other issues—the people-pleasing, the overconsumption of everything, the work ethic, the unresolved trauma, and my narcissistic fleas. I'm not even remotely the same person as when this journey began. I just wish my mother were here to see it—hopefully, she is, just from above.

A Reverse Kafka Revisited

The heaviness I felt in recent months has left me. My dark night of the soul has finally ended. My life has gone through an unparalleled level of purging in recent months. Friends, lovers, jobs, and money have left me. My wants and needs have been re-prioritized. I am a different person than I was seven months ago. I haven't even met this version of myself yet.

My two friendships with my two closest girlfriends ended in recent months. The last few months have been dark, heavy, and morose. Instead of friends offering support, everyone just kept wanting a piece of me, when I didn't even have enough for me. Similar to sharks devouring chum in the water, everyone was coming to take a bite, and then they were surprised when I bit back. I needed their support, not more requests for favors. I needed a shoulder to cry on, not judgment over my new way of life. I needed compassion, not criticism. But all I got was toxicity and one-sided relationships. I was accused of buying my success, my friends, and my looks. These are friends no one needs.

I had persevered through seven years of my life without shedding a single tear. This is not something to brag about. Stuffing your feelings into a suitcase inside your heart only comes back to haunt you later. My father died, I moved out of my hometown, I lost Killian, Paula, and Monica. I quit my job and had to cut up my credit cards. I had to reevaluate every aspect of my life, and it came with a heavy cost. This was worse than a rock bottom; this was spiritual desolation. It feels like global depression, but when depression ends, your life is still the same. When the dark night of the soul ends, you are a different person and better for it.

I began quilting as an at-home therapy activity and grew to love it quickly. Picking out the fabrics, finding the patterns, and sewing the quilt brought me immediate satisfaction and helped me through this darkest period of my life. Focusing on the task at hand allowed me to take my mind off the mistakes the past and the anxiety over my future. Just concentrating on the methodical tapping of the machine was soothing in a dull, monotonous way. My quilts were works of art that I donated to charities.

The financial crisis I was enduring was escalating fast, and my hobbies helped to alleviate my sky-is-falling mindset. Credit cards were shredded, and a spartan budget may have been difficult to adjust to, but was sorely needed.

I was going back to basics. Focus on my essential needs of sleep, food, and connection was needed before I could be of any use to anyone in a relationship. Embracing simplicity was leading to the peace I had been seeking.

My ego was right-sizing. My past accomplishments had left me too arrogant, and my limitations had left me feeling critical. I was either flying too close to the sun or had the self-esteem of used bubble gum. I needed an accurate perspective. I've gone from being a strung-out doctor shopper, to a quilter who helps impoverished kids. Yes, I haven't even met myself yet.

Once the tears came, they just didn't stop. Every Shakespearean-level tragedy I endured was pushed aside in the name of appearing less needy. My needs were unimportant, I had always been shown; my tears were locked away for years before they surfaced. But once they did, they came out with a vengeance. My mother is no longer around, but I can't escape her because I became her. Now that I'm the most mentally healthy I've ever been, I have much more gratitude for mother than I ever had. I've learned from her mistakes and inherited her kind spirit.

As suddenly as my dark night appeared, it faded into the background. A new and improved life appeared on the horizon. Enough time had passed in sobriety, so that I was employable again, my home was beautiful, and new, healthy friendships were starting to form. I felt like a rebuilt engine. Better than the factory model, more streamlined too. Now, when people want a ride, I'm much more discerning as to whom I let in. I was there for everyone, but when I needed someone, they scattered, as cockroaches do when the kitchen light comes on. The hostility, aggression, melancholy, and despair that showed up during this period made me feel as if I myself were no better than a cockroach.

A balanced look at my life tells me this isn't true. I've come out the other side better, stronger, and more spiritual. If I could stay sober through this, I could stay sober through anything. A decade of drinking, drugging, and amoral behavior is now as distant as it ever will be, and my materialism has disappeared. The best things in life are free, as they say. Honesty, integrity, loyalty, compassion, and love—these are all free. I possess all of them now, but I didn't just a short time ago. My reverse Kafka is complete...for now.

Confident Humility

Definition:
Approaching a situation with your ego in check. Not boastful of your achievements, nor embarrassed by your deficiencies. Your ego being just right is confident humility.

Exemplification of Usage:
"Thank you for the promotion; I'm sure you won't be disappointed. I will approach this new position with confident humility to be sure the job is done well."

A warning to Icarus, as he stretched out his wings for the first time: "Don't fly too close to the sun or water. One will melt the wax; the other will weigh down the feathers. Keep to the middle course."

My entire life has been a quest for that middle ground. Coming of age in the eighties, when the motto was "Too much is never enough," certainly didn't help. More is not better; balance is better. When to rest, when to work. When to have fun, when to clean. The purging of unbalanced friendships, rejecting a value system that no longer served me, addressing my issues from childhood, and shedding toxic romantic partnerships have finally allowed me to find this middle ground.

My arrogance during my tenure as a well-paid teacher and the quest for more material items and fun times led me down a path to self-destruction. Like the story of David and Goliath, it was the little things that led to my downfall. A small bottle of pills, a six-pack of beer, and small, unnecessary purchases every day became vices so large they led to my downfall. My arrogance was the size of Goliath. It blindsided me to the "small" issues that were my David, my downfall. The little things in life *are* the big things, however. A sunrise after heartbreak, a warm cup of coffee on a cold day, a smile from your kids—these are little things on which to focus. This balance has led to a slow and steady "win the race" attitude, in contrast to my life of jackrabbit starts followed by long periods of burnout.

Three changes in attitude—being comfortable saying no, developing a routine that works for me, and eliminating the habit of comparing myself to others—altered the course, consistency, and quality of my life. This snowballed into finding my life's purpose and happiness within. I adopted discipline in my life, something I truly never had. I reevaluated my romantic relationships, realizing that

I never truly had a partner who had the same value system. I found men whom I dated were fixer-uppers; after eliminating that toxic habit, I directed that fixer-upper attitude toward myself, which has earned the highest return. Never again will I allow a job, a lover, or a girlfriend to lead me astray from my core values of education, volunteer work, pacifism, and purity of heart and spirit. Staying true to your values leads to genuine, deep connections.

I began to be comfortable saying no, being assertive, and having to be fine with whatever fallout happened when my people-pleasing stopped. It wasn't fair to me or to the people I was helping. People-pleasing can be a form of manipulation. A rescuing-victim mindset can easily shift to a persecuting-victim mindset. Sometimes help is often no help at all. Frank was the kind of help no one needed. It was the help I never received that I needed the most.

My dark night of the soul—when friends came looking for favors even though I could barely help myself—forced difficult conversations. When I realized that half of the friends I had periodically helped couldn't even be bothered to buy me a cup of coffee or give me a hug, I was forced to reevaluate those friendships. I could no longer cross an ocean for people who couldn't be bothered to cross a puddle for me. That would only lead to anger and resentment, which could lead to a relapse, and they were not worth my sobriety. Guess what? The world did not end when I lost friends. In fact, it became more peaceful in the absence of their unnecessary drama in my life.

I no longer cared if they liked or valued me, no longer cared if I was likable. I was more concerned with being respected and valued. Loyalty, trust, and respect are like the three points of a triangle. You lose one, and you lose all three. Once I realized that those friends didn't respect me, the loyalty was gone. Once I realized I couldn't trust them to have my back in a crisis, the respect was gone. Once the loyalty was gone, their absence didn't make a difference. I used to water myself down, put myself on clearance so they could afford me. Now I'm okay with not being everyone's cup of tea. In fact, not being everyone's cup of tea is my best quality.

I stopped comparing myself to others. I course corrected toward my North Star. I was unconcerned with who had more than I did, and instead was grateful that I had more than I did the previous year. I was unconcerned that my bank account wasn't larger, and instead was grateful my current income could pay my bills and keep me fed. I was unconcerned that I didn't have the fanciest vacations or designer clothes, as the price tag for that lifestyle was outside of my core values anyway. Instead, I was grateful for matching socks and a weekend with my children. I decided to stop waiting for happiness and serenity, and instead created it myself.

Eliminating nonreciprocal relationships and the need to have the best of everything had the result of freeing up copious amounts of time, our most valuable asset. With this time, I created routines that worked for me. My house, my health, my finances became more organized. I'd rather have four quarters than twenty nickels—the "fewer friends is more" attitude freed up time for me. Time I desperately needed to rise from rock bottom. Time to rebuild my career, time for my hobbies, time for self-care, time for my kids—in short, time for things that really matter. The "less is more," the "little things are the big things," and the "peace is more important than a boyfriend" attitudes became the foundation for my balanced, organized, purpose-driven life.

The foundation of my friendships and other relationships had been shaky for some time. I liken the quality of human connections to the structure of a tree. Some are like leaves—only around during the sunshine. Many are like branches—snapping when you try to lean on them. I. needed connections that were as strong as the trunk of a tree, which is strong and lasts a very long time. By working on myself, I strengthened my own tree trunk and made it less likely that I ever needed to lean on others. By becoming a solid oak tree, I will hopefully attract other oak trees. Birds of a feather flock together. When *I* was as reliable as a maple leaf in the summer, I attracted maple leaves that flew away in a storm. But when I'm an oak tree with solid branches and bountiful acorns, that's what I will attract.

Part of working on myself involved returning to the importance of hobbies in my life. I had always loved reading—thanks, Mom! I began to read again, I began to scrapbook again, and I started hiking with friends. During one of my shopping sprees while I was with Frank, I purchased a sewing machine, many yards of fabric, and some patterns. I decided to haul all of that out of the closet and put it to good use. I got on the Internet and watched sewing tutorial videos. In no time, I was not just sewing, but quilting. I created twelve specialty quilts in my first year of quilting. I donated half to charitable organizations for auction and gave the other half as presents. I fully intend to buy a body form and explore making some of my own clothes.

I've always been outside the mainstream in terms of, well, everything, and now that I'm embracing it, I might as well take my creative talents to another level. My sober powers have brought me nothing but enjoyment. I'm no longer watering down my authenticity.

Once enough time had passed, I was able to return to teaching and was hired by a local trade school. My work experience could not have been a more perfect fit. The position required a master's degree, science-classroom experience, and above-average car knowledge. Check on all three. The return to the classroom was exciting, to say the least. It's an exceptionally impressive campus, relaxed working atmosphere, and above-average pay. Almost immediately, I established a great rapport with my students and colleagues. It is the perfect fit. My purpose in life as a teacher, quilter, writer, mom, and friend were now solidly reestablished.

Once I started valuing myself, I began attracting more things of value into my life. Once I was grateful for the pain, I began to feel joy. Once I appreciated the little things in life, bigger things began to appear. Once I embraced my authentic self, I glowed from within and repelled people who embraced their darkness. Toxic people no longer felt comfortable even approaching me. Drama faded; serenity appeared. The biggest shitstorm I had ever been through seems to be producing a rainbow that extends forever.

At the end of this rainbow is genuine happiness. Not giddy happiness, but content happiness, which is better. It lasts longer; it's sustainable. The fun, the prosperity, the love—what I had been chasing, but had always eluded me. Once I slowed down long enough to heal, correct my own toxic behaviors, and be grateful for everything I had, blessings upon blessings and true happiness came to find me.

I no longer chase anything. I have everything I need within my home, head, heart, and soul. I can now self-correct to avoid flying too close to the sun or going so low as to crash into the water. My wings are solid now, and it's my time to fly. And when I'm tired, I have a solid oak trunk upon which to rest my weary head. A solid oak tree, wings, a never-ending rainbow—the meek woman everyone once knew now has an entire Earth to her name. I've built a life I don't need a vacation from, and that is the best present I could ever give myself.

"The meek shall inherit the Earth."
(Matthew 5:3–11)

Appendix
Comorbidities Do
Not Travel Alone

Your addiction is an external attempt to solve an internal problem. As we have seen, there are a multitude of underlying conditions that may exist, and often there is more than one. For instance, in my case, I had unresolved childhood trauma and PTSD from my second marriage. In addition to that, I have bipolar disorder. The good news is that, in working with my therapist, I have processed my trauma, and now I am on a medication schedule that minimizes the impact of the bipolar disorder. Currently, it is stable. By resolving these issues, I've cut the need for a drug of choice off at the source. Adding to that, by publishing this book and developing the hobbies of reading, quilting, and scrapbooking, I have found healthy coping mechanisms to use during future times of stress. I also use the sobriety program Breaking the Chains, which fosters self-love, authenticity, and self-empowerment.

I have included graphics on bipolar disorder and autism, as well as statistics on domestic abuse. These are for illustrative purposes only in terms of enlightening anyone struggling with addiction and helping them identify their co-morbid conditions. The final analysis of that, of course, should be addressed with a therapist, psychiatrist, or family physician.

***

Domestic violence is a major issue in the US and around the world; many nonprofit organizations work tirelessly to provide critical support and services to survivors. Every year, more than 10 million men and women in the US are subjected to domestic violence. Its impact can be felt far and wide.

1. More than 1 in 3 women (35.6%) and more than 1 in 4 men (28.5%) in the US will experience rape, physical violence, and/or stalking by an intimate partner in their lifetime ("Domestic Violence Statistics," National Domestic Violence Hotline, Accessed, https://www.thehotline.org/stakeholders/domestic-violence-statistics/).

2. Nearly 20 people per minute are physically abused by an intimate partner in the United States. During one year, this adds up to more than 10 million women and men ("Statistics,"

NCADV, Accessed, https://ncadv.org/statistics/).

3. Approximately 1 in 4 women and 1 in 7 men have experienced severe physical violence by an intimate partner during their lifetime (Ibid., Accessed).

4. Intimate-partner violence accounts for 15% of all violent crimes ("Some Statistics about Domestic Violence, "Project Sanctuary, Accessed, https://www.projectsanctuary.org/dv/some-statistics-about-domestic-violence/).

5. On a typical day, there are more than 20,000 phone calls placed to domestic-violence hotlines nationwide (Ibid., Accessed).

6. Worldwide, almost one-third (27%) of women aged 15–49 years who have been in a relationship report that they have been subjected to some form of physical and/or sexual violence by their intimate partner ("Violence against Women," World Health Organization, Accessed, https://www.who.int/news-room/fact-sheets/detail/violence-against-women/).

7. Approximately 1 in 4 gay men, 1 in 3 bisexual men, and 3 in 10 heterosexual men will experience rape, physical violence, and/or stalking by

an intimate partner in their lifetime ("Domestic Violence, Statistics, and Facts," safehorizon, Accessed, https://www.safehorizon.org/get-informed/domestic-violence-statistics-facts/#statistics-and-facts/).

8. Approximately 44% of lesbian women and 61% of bisexual women experience rape, physical violence, or stalking by an intimate partner ("Frequently Asked Questions about Domestic Violence and Firearms," American Progress, Accessed, https://www.americanprogress.org/article/frequently-asked-questions-domestic-violence-firearms/).

9. Nearly 2 in 5 transgender people report having experienced intimate-partner violence or other forms of coercive control and/or physical harm (Ibid., Accessed).

10. Most cases of domestic violence are never reported to the police ("Domestic Violence Statistics," Shelter House, Accessed, http://www.shelterhousenwfl.org/resources/domestic-violence-statistics/).

11. In domestic-violence homicides, women are six times more likely to be killed when a gun is in the house ("Some Statistics about Domestic Violence," Project Sanctuary, Accessed, https://

www.projectsanctuary.org/dv/some-statistics-about-domestic-violence/).

12. Approximately 1 in 15 children are exposed to intimate-partner violence each year, and 90% of these children are eyewitnesses to this violence ("Statistics," NCADV, Accessed, https://ncadv.org/STATISTICS).

13. Almost half (47.5%) of American Indian/ Alaska Native women, 45.1% of non-Hispanic Black women, 37.3% of non-Hispanic White women, 34.4% of Hispanic women, and 18.3% of Asian-Pacific Islander women experience contact sexual violence, physical violence, and/or stalking by an intimate partner in their lifetime ("Domestic Violence, Statistics, and Facts," safehorizon, Accessed, https://www.safehorizon.org/get-informed/domestic-vio-lence-statistics-facts/#statistics-and-facts/).

14. Globally as many as 38% of all murders of women are committed by intimate partners ("Violence against Women," World Health Organization, Accessed, https://www.who.int/news-room/fact-sheets/detail/violence-against-women/).

15. Women with disabilities have a 40% greater risk of intimate-partner violence, especially

severe violence, than women without disabilities ("Intimate Partner Violence: Know the Risks and What You Can Do to Help Yourself," American Psychological Association, Accessed on, https://www.apa.org/topics/physical-abuse-violence/intimate-partner/).

16. Approximately 53% of battered women still involved with the perpetrator experienced self-blame for causing the violence ("Missing 20-Year-Old Female, NR23743dm," Los Angeles Police Department, Accessed on, https://www.lapdonline.org/).

17. Approximately 63% of homeless women have experienced domestic violence in their adult lives ("Domestic Violence and Homelessness," National Coalition for the Homeless, Accessed on, https://www.nationalhomeless.org/fact-sheets/domestic.html/).

18. Approximately 1 in 5 **female high school students** reports being physically and/or sexually abused by a dating partner ("Intimate Partner Violence: Know the Risks and What You Can Do to Help Yourself," American Psychological Association, Accessed on, https://www.apa.org/topics/physical-abuse-violence/intimate-partner/).

19. A study shows that the lifetime economic cost of intimate-partner violence in the US population is **$3.6 trillion** (National Network to End Domestic Violence, Accessed on, https://nnedv.org/).

20. On average, more than 3 women and 1 man are murdered by their intimate partners in the US every day ("Domestic Violence Statistics," Shelter House, Accessed, http://www.shelterhousenwfl.org/resources/domestic-violence-statistics).

The numbers may be staggering, but so many great organizations are working to end domestic violence and support its survivors.

Apricot for Victims Services was built specifically for the needs of violence survivors' providers, making it simple to manage program enrollment, hotline calls, shelter services, court services, visitor logs, and more. In addition, AVS case management software has forms and reports that can be customized to meet funder requirements, including compliance with VAWA and VOCA.

If you or someone you know is a victim of domestic violence, call the National Domestic Violence Hotline at 1–800–799–7233 or visit their website *to chat online 24/7.*

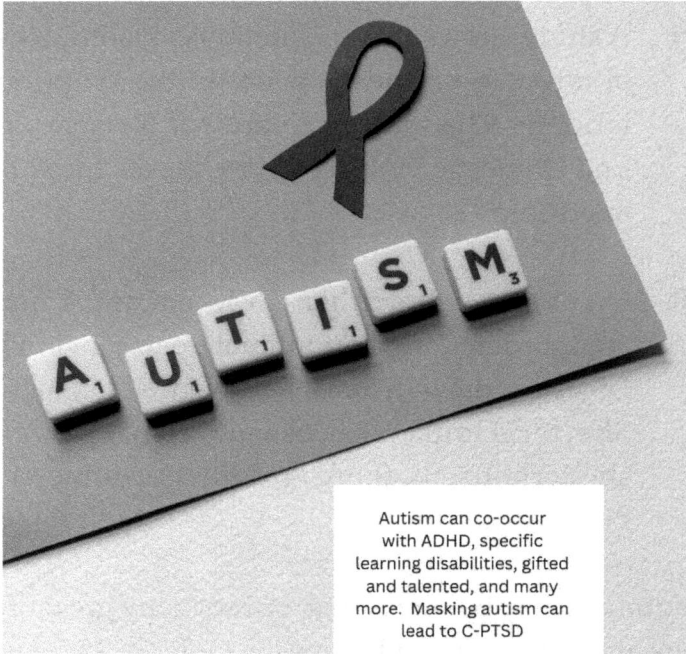

Autism can co-occur with ADHD, specific learning disabilities, gifted and talented, and many more. Masking autism can lead to C-PTSD

Image Sources: https://drprbhuyan.com/treatments/autism-spectrum-disorders

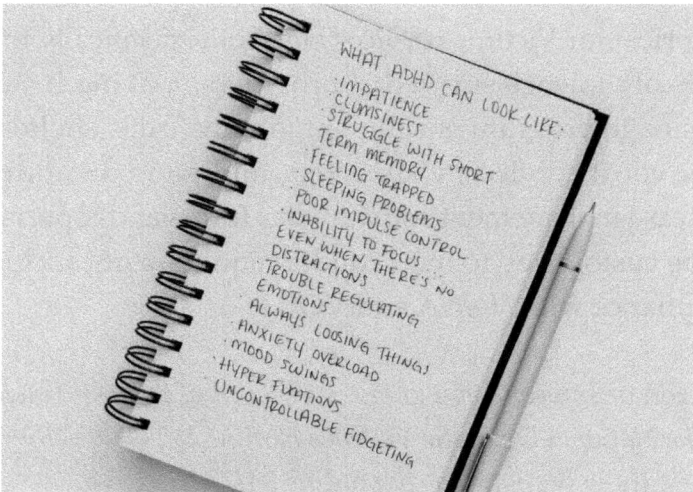

WHAT ADHD CAN LOOK LIKE:
- IMPATIENCE
- CLUMSINESS
- STRUGGLE WITH SHORT TERM MEMORY
- FEELING TRAPPED
- SLEEPING PROBLEMS
- POOR IMPULSE CONTROL
- INABILITY TO FOCUS EVEN WHEN THERE'S NO DISTRACTIONS
- TROUBLE REGULATING EMOTIONS
- ALWAYS LOOSING THINGS
- ANXIETY OVERLOAD
- MOOD SWINGS
- HYPER FIXATIONS
- UNCONTROLLABLE FIDGETING

Image Sources: https://www.altumhealth.co.uk/adhd-in-adults/

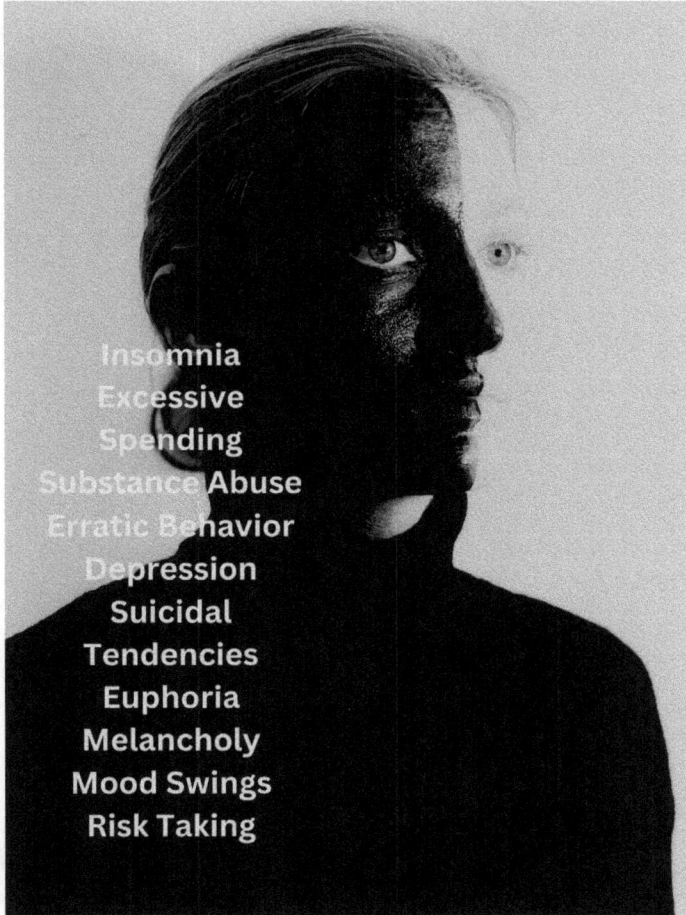

Insomnia
Excessive
Spending
Substance Abuse
Erratic Behavior
Depression
Suicidal
Tendencies
Euphoria
Melancholy
Mood Swings
Risk Taking

Image Sources: https://ericschmiedl.org/2022/07/24/disability-pride-month/